DEAD RECKONINGS

A Review of Horror and the Weird in the Arts
Edited by Alex Houstoun and Michael J. Abolafia

No. 32 (Fall 2022)

DEAD RECKONINGS is published by Hippocampus Press, P.O. Box 641, New York, NY 10156 (www.hippocampuspress. com). Copyright © 2022 by Hippocampus Press. Cover art by Jason C. Eckhardt. Cover design by Barbara Briggs Silbert. Hippocampus Press logo by Anastasia Damianakos. Orders and subscriptions should be sent to Hippocampus Press. Contact Alex Houstoun at deadreckoningsjournal@gmail.com for assignments or before submitting a publication for review.

ISSN 1935-6110   ISBN 9781614983972

Can You Dig It?

Daniel Pietersen

AMARA THORNTON and KATY SOAR, ed., *Strange Relics: Stories of Archeology and the Supernatural, 1895–1954.* United Kingdom: Handheld Press, 2022. 195 pp. £12.99 tpb. ISBN: 9781912766581.

One of the most immediately striking things about Handheld Press's library of weird collections and anthologies has been its consistently excellent design work. From the quietly mournful imagery of *The Villa and The Vortex* to the raging, atavistic monster that roars from the cover of *British Weird,* each book has pursued the publisher's consistent, minimalist approach while still ensuring that each entry in the series has its own, distinct character.

Strange Relics is no different. A sly, smirking satyr leers out at the prospective reader with its drowsy eyelids half-closed and a knowing curl to its full lips. It takes a moment to realise that the stark white spaces which break up the creature's gray-scale features are human feet clad in dainty, Grecian sandals and perhaps a moment more to understand that the satyr is in fact part of a floor-tile; unearthly life glimmering from cold stone.

It's a wonderful image and one that beautifully illustrates *Strange Relic*'s archeological concerns—how ancient things can hold more than simply a memory of the past—but it is also a piece of weird archeology in itself. When Dorothy Quick's "The Cracks of Time" was published in the September 1948 issue of *Weird Tales*—alongside work by the likes of August Derleth, Mary Elizabeth Counselman and Clark Ashton Smith—it was prefaced with this eerie illustration, credited to the artist Boris Dolgov. This in itself isn't unusual; stories in *Weird Tales* often benefited from illustration and Dolgov was a prolific contributor, with three works in that September issue alone. What is unusual is that Dolgov appears to have never existed. We have no biographical detail beyond some anecdotes or half-memories and no mention of that name appears in contemporary censuses. Some believe that Dolgov may actually have been a gestalt persona that allowed multiple artists to collaborate or even a pseudonym of Dolgov's fellow illustrator Hannes Bok. All of this is possible—pulp artists often used pseudonyms for various reasons (Hannes Bok, in fact, is a pseudonym for Wayne Francis Woodard)—but, ultimately, we will probably never know who Boris Dolgov was or if he even existed. Like the satyr in his illustration he smiles out at us from history, knowing that we will never know.

All of which is a long-winded way to second Thornton and Soar's introduction, where they explain how archeology is not just a literal "study of ancient things" but a way to look at how the present encounters the ancient past and how "through these encounters the barrier between the present and the past becomes thin." Archeology, for the two editors, is not simply the uncovering of a dead past but the allowing of knowledge, and failures of knowledge, back into the present; it is a work of haunting, opening a door onto the places and people and practices of the past. And doors, often, work both ways.

This act of haunting can be as subtle as it is in "Through the Veil" by Arthur Conan Doyle, where simply lingering in one of these thin places allows the spirits of a young couple to intersect and overlap with their possible ancestors, little more than a wisp of memory that nonetheless opens up "wider horizons." In John Buchan's "Ho! The Merry Masons," however, the haunting becomes much more predatory and malevolent. The sallow-faced Leithen expresses the opinion of how some intense event or emotion could have "left an indelible mark on the ether" and then supports this with a tale where he "seemed to be looking into a gulf of unimaginable evil." Buchan, in a way which anticipates *The Stone Tape* of Nigel Kneale, peels back layers of embedded tradition until he reveals the blood and bone of "things aeons removed from the common trivial wickedness of mankind." The final section—in which Leithen, his consciousness already weakened and made susceptible by a recent concussion, lies near death—is a masterful piece of cosmic, vertiginous horror. This idea of gazing in only to find that something is gazing back reappears in "The Cracks of

Time," which we've already encountered briefly. Here Dorothy Quick begins her story with a startling opening line: "It was when the cocktail party I was giving for Myra was at its height that I first saw the face." The face is that of the satyr which graces the book's cover and Quick's narrator, Sheila, tells how what begins as a vague impression caused by shadows and cracks on a floor tile becomes "a living, throbbing thing, marvellous beyond human knowing." Like Nora in Algernon Blackwood's "Roman Remains," also included in the volume, Sheila first becomes the satyr's conspirator and then his thrall as he's revealed to be Pan himself. Eventually, as a woman trapped in a failing marriage and surrounded by friends she cares little for, Sheila is consumed by panic in its original sense; the wild, animal terror felt by those in lonely places. Sheila's eventual fate is not unexpected but it's striking for how easily, how willingly she accepts it.

No anthology of archeological weird could be complete without a contribution from M. R. James and it's to Thornton and Soar's credit that, rather than the more obvious "Oh, Whistle and I'll Come To You, My Lad" or even "A Warning to the Curious," they've selected "A View from a Hill" to be in *Strange Relics*. This reflects the decision outlined in the introduction to move away from tales of "that-which-should-be-left-buried" to "encounters with the material remains of the past." In James's tale of sinister alchemy and the perils of disturbing the unquiet dead, those material remains are shown to be far more literal than we might at first imagine. Arthur Machen, another obvious name when it comes to tales of atavism and strange remnants, takes this even further with "The Shining Pyramid," in which the past literally is still alive, hiding in the hollows and hills that the age of cars and electricity rarely touches. As with many stories about otherness and prior times, though, Machen succumbs to the temptation of aligning that otherness with an incomprehensible evil; the description of his "little people" as having "dusky limbs" and "almond eyes burning with evil and unspeakable lusts" speaks to a more modern-day prejudice. Yet this again is a kind of archeology. The past doesn't care about our opinion of it and it is up to us alone to decide which of its "material remains" we praise and which we condemn.

Strange Relics is yet another excellent anthology in Handheld's run of weird writing and the editors' selection of tales, some old favourites but many less well-known pieces like Rose Macaulay's slight but still-chilling "Whitewash," is only heightened by their overarching philosophy of what archeology is and how it can be used to reflect on one of the key elements of horror—is it worse for things to end prematurely or for them to persist beyond their allotted span?

A Newly Arrived Triumph

Géza A. G. Reilly

ATTILA VERES. *The Black Maybe: Liminal Tales*. Translated by Luca Karafiáth. Richmond, VA: Valancourt Books, 2022. 310 pp. $29.99 hc. ISBN: 9781954321694; $17.99 tpb. ISBN: 9781954321700.

It is always a pleasure to find a new and exciting author, though in the case of Attila Veres, it would perhaps be better to say that he is newly *arrived*. Veres has been writing for several years in both Norway and his native Hungary, working in film and television along with publishing a successful novel and short story collection. *The Black Maybe: Liminal Tales* is Veres' first collection to be printed in English. As his first English work (and only his second published collection), *The Black Maybe* is a resounding success for the young author. Though not every story is a total triumph, devotees of weird fiction would be well served by paying attention to Veres' work.

The prose in *The Black Maybe* is crisp and precise throughout, never wasting words on overly verbose description and never skimping on the necessary moments of atmosphere and character that give horror fiction its power. Special mention must be made of Veres' translator, Luca Karafiáth. Hungarian and English are vastly different languages, and it is often difficult to translate from one to the other without losing the text's thrust and power. Yet, nowhere in *The Black Maybe* is there any sense that the text was not composed by a native speaker of English. Throughout, Veres' writing carries with it a deep sense of dreadful anticipation, occasional humor, and realistic dialogue.

At their best, Veres' stories present characters in the midst of deeply disturbing, often arcane, scenarios. In "To Bite a Dog," that scenario is more philosophical than it is magical, and the locating of this narrative during the recent pandemic brings an immediacy and desperation to the piece that makes it resonate with we survivors. In "Fogtown," Veres plays with nostalgia and the form of traditional narratives to present a surreal scenario that has a powerful emotional impact. And in "Multiplied by Zero," Veres shows us how deeply strange a typical office worker of no outstanding merit might become in order to find respite in nihilistic obliteration.

Surprisingly, Veres seems as adept at dark comedy as he is at the weird and unsettling. "Multiplied by Zero" is one such story with a comedic bent, though there the humor is as sharp and cutting as a razor blade. "Sky Filled With Crows, Then Nothing At All" is replete with humor, though the sentimental bent to this demon-infused morality tale causes it to avoid tipping over into full comedy–to its betterment and the surprise of the reader. And, though it might say more about me as a reader than anything else, I found a good amount of humor in "Walks Among You." Though, again, the humor holds a philosophic purpose and is not without a dark, satirical drive behind it.

Though there is no real sign that Veres wants to create an overarching fictional universe in his stories, several are still linked by references both specific and oblique. "Multiplied by Zero" and "Walks Among You" are explicitly connected, for example. This is perhaps not surprising, given that those are the two stories where Lovecraft's influence on Veres is felt most strongly. However, both "The Amber Complex" and "Fogtown" are also explicitly linked without any outside influence seemingly upon them. If anything drives those narratives as a unit, it is a sense of deep and abiding desperation for what was once a possibility but cannot now be grasped.

Those readers with little knowledge of Hungarian history or culture will not find themselves at sea in this collection. Veres' writing is grounded in the soil of his mother nation, but it is not dependent on what nourishes it. There were only two elements that a non-Hungarian might be confused by, and neither of those were critical. To set potential readers at ease, "pálinka" is a traditional brandy much enjoyed in Hungary, and the "generational trauma" (p. 183) caused by the death of Prime Minister József Antall being announced during a *Duck Tales* cartoon did, in fact, lead to the creation of a flashbulb memory (and, later, an actual psychological issue) for a wide swath of Hungarians. Though the stories in *The Black Maybe* are rooted in Hungary, they are effortlessly understood by those from different shores.

So why, then, are these *liminal* tales, exactly? It seems to me that Veres' narratives focus on two sorts of scenarios: characters who have been pushed to the margins of the world for one reason or another, or settings that fall far outside the norm of prosaic life despite still being part of the world at large. Veres never falls into the temptation of treating the former like puppets upon a sadistic stage, nor does he allow the latter to become nothing more than terrible place set dressings where no solace can be found. Indeed, there is beauty and sympathy throughout *The Black Maybe*, and perhaps that is the most remarkable quality of the collection. Horrific events abound, and awful people populate many of these pages, but the nostalgic, often surreal actions they carry out or fall victim to are rarely, if ever, presented with a sense that these people, these locations, are far removed from us and the spaces we call home.

It may be the case (and thankfully so) that we will never find ourselves confronting the reality of "The Midnight School" or in the nightmarishly hallucinatory spa of "In the Snow, Sleeping." And yet, with *The Black Maybe*, Veres makes us remember the beliefs that we were raised with, the horrific encounters we've had, the music and nightlife we've been drawn to, and the desire to escape the banal uniformity we've occasionally been trapped in. Further, he reminds us that these moments, however slight–however liminal–are nonetheless significant. Sometimes monstrously so, but always remarkably.

The Black Maybe is hopefully not the last volume of Attila Veres' work translated into and published in English. It receives a hearty recommendation from me if for no other reason than the selfish fact that I want to see more from this talented author–and that means getting as many as I can to read what he's offered us thus far. Pick up *The Black Maybe*– you won't be disappointed.

June Ruins Everything

June Pulliam

Because I do. That's another way of alerting you, dear reader, that thar be spoilers here. I can't always weigh my judgment on what's streaming right now without revealing a bit of the plot. Just sit back and relax while I ruin some of your favorite horror and dystopian television so you can avoid the worst and find the best.

The Worst.

Westworld, Season 4 • HBO

I really loved seasons 1 and 2 of HBO's *Westworld*, a high-concept reimagining of Michael Crichton's 1973 film of the same name. Season 3 was a little plodding but wrapped up the story with the now sentient and loose-in-the-world androids infiltrating the human race, intent on destroying a dataset controlling them that still existed on a massive hard drive. Season 4, however, is a hopelessly tangled narrative that requires a scorecard to keep track of. Multiple long tracking shots reveal weeping synthetic lifeforms mumbling prophecies of doom. The synthetic lifeforms believe they are human, or they're not in on the joke: it just depends. Characters that were formally human are now *also* synthetic lifeforms: both exist in the show's timeline. Synthetic lifeforms destroy more humans, as well as each other. There's a lot of shooting, and Aaron Paul has grown a beard, runs around a lot, and looks confused. I get it: androids are smarter than humans, but they are also like us because messy emotions. But I have lost interest in these characters, who are just too hard to keep track of.

A long-running series doesn't have to conclude this way. HBO's *Game of Thrones* had an obvious narrative arc that is heading towards something, and its characters were fully developed individuals. What happens with synthetic life becomes sentient? *Picard* does it better with Lt. Commander Data, as does *Her* (2013), *Ex Machina* (2014) or even the Terminator series and *Robocop* (1987) and of course Phillip K. Dick's "Do Androids Dream of Electric Sheep" and the two Blade Runner films based on it. Season 4 of *Westworld* tries to pass off sloppy writing as complex and cutting edge. If you decide to skip this season, you won't be missing anything.

The Walking Dead, Season 11.

The Walking Dead is still on the air. Zombies are everywhere. Most of the characters you loved in the beginning of this series are now dead or not part of the story any longer. Just a few remaining long-term characters continue to learn again and again that humans are the worst! Way worse than zombies. Did I say that this show is still on the air? And that it has also spawned several spin offs? That AMC has a whole sub-The Walking Dead channel? Am I a zombie, watching the same things play out over and over again?

Production of *The Walking Dead* was suspended for a year due to the pandemic, and when it finally returned, current events had changed how we think about the zombie apocalypse. After living through a pandemic, a coup attempt, and five hurricanes in one year in a world where half of the country no longer believes in facts and the threat of nuclear war is as high as it was during the Cuban Missile Crisis, a zombie apocalypse just feels redundant. Now *TWD's* showrunners say that Rick will not return for the season finale—he is instead to star in one of the newer spin-offs. Can't say I blame him. I am just exhausted by this show with its uneven writing and refashioning of the same old conflicts season after season. Yawn.

Better.

American Horror Stories, Season 2 • FX

The last season of *American Horror Story* was so bad that I couldn't watch it all the way through. The show's creators had just flat run out of ideas: *1984* was a sad leftover casserole of earlier themes. So you can understand why, when Brian Murphy and Ryan Falchuk's *American Horror Stories* dropped, I did not immediately watch it.

That was a mistake. *Stories* works because it's an anthology show rather than an anthology series along the model of *Story*. Each season of *Story* is a mash-up of related horror tropes and subgenres, such as the combination of screen vampires, serial killers, and ghosts in *Hotel*. Each episode of *American Horror Stories*, however, stands alone. While some episodes riff on characters from *American Horror Story*, others are truly original. Case in point: Episodes 4 and 5: "Milkmaids" and "Bloody Mary," both loosely based on Mercy Brown, a 19-year-old Rhode Island who died of consumption and was exhumed when people suspected that she was a vampire and the Bloody Mary myth respectively. "Milkmaids" is far more interesting than the actual facts surrounding Mercy Brown, while "Bloody Mary" is notable in how the story focuses exclusively on contemporary Black characters. The AHS franchise always aces the Bechdel Test, which asks whether a film features at least two named women characters who talk to each other about something other than a man: women of different ages, races, abilities, and body types have starring, recurring roles. However, while there several some notable stories in this season, the writing is uneven. But at least you can pick and choose episodes to watch rather than having to invest in the whole series before deciding if it was worth your time or not.

The Best.

What We Do in the Shadows, Season 4 • FX

If you aren't watching this show, what's wrong with you? *What We Do in the Shadows* is one of the best comedies ever. *What We Do in the Shadows* takes its name from a 2014 film of the same name, but the similarities end there. Hulu's *WWDITS* follows four vampires who have been living on Staten Island for the past century as they try to fit in with the locals while feeding on them. Fortunately, Staten Island is part of New York City, so they their eclectic way of dressing and speaking is barely noticed by humans. In Season 4, Nandor the Relentless (Kayvan Novak), Nadja (Natasha Demetriou) and Lazlo Cravensworth (Matt Berry), and Colin Robinson (Mark Proksch), have found their own interests, the Vampiric Residence gets a makeover, and Nandor's long-suffering human familiar Guillermo (Harvey Guillen) is sick of everyone' shit.

In this season, energy vampire Colin Robinson, who died at the end of Season 3, is reborn, and Lazlo raises him from infancy to adulthood in the space of a year. Baby Colin Robinson becomes a show-tune singing sensation in Nadja's vampire nightclub, which becomes deader than the vampires after Colin loses his voice to puberty. Guillermo finally comes out to his family as gay (which they already knew and were fine with) as well as someone who lives with vampires and aspires to be one (which more difficult for them to accept as they are all descendants of vampire killer Abraham Ven Helsing). Simon the Devious steals Lazlo's cursed witch's hat by creating an HGTV-type home remodeling show. After being a widow for over a thousand years, Nandor remarries, then quickly becomes bored by his new wife because she is too agreeable. Nandor, Lazlo, and Colin have an encounter with the Jersey Devil. Somebody gets the brain scramblies. And Nandor accidentally steals Guillermo's boyfriend. This is the last straw for Guillermo, who in the season finale, realizes that Nandor will never honor his vague promises to make him a vampire, so he leaves and bribes a young and less successful vampire to make him immortal. And Lazlo sings a song from Fiddler on the Roof while accompanying himself on the piano in the season finale (Matt Berry is a gifted singer as well as a comic genius). I'm really hoping that Guillermo returns to Season 5 as a vampire because I can't wait to see what happens when a vampire-killing prodigy becomes the thing that he is so good at killing.

As per usual, this season continues the show's running gags and begins some new ones. The dialogue is full of witty one-liners and deadpan non-sequiturs. Celebrities who have played famous vampires in movies, including those from Jemaine Clement and Taika Waititi's 2014 film, appear as their characters. And the vampires continue to become more relatable humans not so much through their grief over the ephemeral nature of life, but through their propinquity to do the stupidest thing possible in nearly every situation. This is a show that you will return to over and over because you cannot possibly catch all of the running gags and Easter eggs in one viewing, and also, because it's just damn funny.

Interview with the Vampire, Season 1 • AMC

It's a shame that Anne Rice did not live long enough to see AMC's adaption of her novel into a series. She collaborated on the production with the show's producers: the result, a version that is both faithful to her novel as well as an improvement on it. This is not Neil Jordan's 1994 film, with its asexual representation of Rice's homoerotic vampires. These vampires are able to do something more than just brood about their feelings. After Lestat turns Louis, the pair engage in passionate fucking and fighting in Storyville. In this version, Lestat (Sam Reid) meets his Louis (Jacob Anderson) in New Orleans *after* the Civil War. Also, Louis de Pointe du Lac is, appropriately, a Creole, not the white planter played by Brad Pitt in Jordan's film. While the de Pointe du Lac family's original wealth came from their plantation, in 1910 when Louis first meets Lestat, he keeps his mother and siblings in the style to which they are accustomed to investing the family assets into several brothels in Storyville, the infamous red-light district of New Orleans. AMC has also revised the character Claudia, the vampire daughter that Lestat makes for Louis: Bailey Bass who plays Claudia is not the little girl of Rice's version, but a petite teen. This change is important in how it allows the showrunners to depict Claudia using her sexuality to lure potential victims: Bass looks old enough so that the show's producers aren't publicly condemned for sexualizing children. However, Bass still looks sufficiently young to create stark contrast between her seeming innocence and her "mature" capability violence. The teen Claudia also has an adolescent appetite. While Louis is a "vegetarian" vampire in the style of *Twilight's* Cullen family (mostly feeding off of rats, dogs, and cats rather than humans), Claudia can take several victims a night because her now eternally teen body needs more food.

Eric Bogosian plays interviewer Daniel Molloy, who survived his first attempt to interview Louis in Rice's *Interview*. The present day of AMC's *Interview* is forty years ahead of Rice's, and Daniel is now a well-known journalist, older and frailer, but maybe not wiser. Daniel is interviewing Louis again, at the vampire's invitation, to document his version of events and share them with the world. He still, however, wants to be turned into a vampire, but this time to reverse the ravages of Parkinson's Disease rather than remain forever young.

The season ends with Louis and Claudia "killing" Lestat, who has become increasingly more angry and violent towards the love of his life as he is less able to control his fledglings, who prefer each other's company to his own. But of course, Lestat is not dead because they did not burn the body, and when he reappears in Season 2, there will be hell to pay. (This comes as no surprise to you if you have read Rice's novel).

AMC's *Interview* also does a better job of bringing old New Orleans to life than Rice's novel or Jordan's film not just by the city's *laissez les bons temps rouler* attitude, but its multicultural roots and complex racial structure. During Louis' first twenty odd years as a vampire, he grows increasingly frustrated by life in his hometown as its three-race system is replaced by American Jim Crow segregation of whites and non-whites. Because Louis is now viewed as Black rather than Creole, he must use white intermediaries to conduct business with institutions that are closed to non-whites.

Interview with the Vampire's careful writing, casting, and costuming make this one of my favorite shows this year, and I sincerely hope that AMC doesn't decide to take its show runners to work on another project as they make Season 2 the way they did for the second season of *The Walking Dead* and invested in producing *Mad Men* instead.

I will end this column with a prediction about broader trends in horror fiction and media. After their long run at the beginning of the 21st century, current events have made zombies passe. What *We Do in the Shadows* and *Interview with the Vampire* have both been greenlit by their respective networks for new seasons, and I think their popularity predicts a wider resurgence of the vampire in horror fiction and film.

Ramsey's Rant: The Disengaged

Ramsey Campbell

Creativity can be unmerciful, and you can't hide behind your fiction. The harder you try, the more you may reveal. Just as handwriting can expose traces of immaturity in its owner, however intellectual they may otherwise be, so writing fiction in particular can expose naïveté or worse. The same pitfall can betray even the best-read reader, perhaps because reading doesn't necessarily shape their personality. Although I was so precocious that I read Edith Wharton ("Afterward") when I was six, more than a year later I was perpetrating "Black Fingers from Space". By eleven I was versed in most of the classics of our field—in the 1950s they tended to dominate it, to the extent that I encountered the same stories in anthology after anthology, and felt compelled to reread them every time—but could only write the likes of *Ghostly Tales*, in which I simulated knowledge of a remarkable range of subjects (happily married couples, European castles, Greek islands, occult battles) drawn exclusively from my reading, and not too selectively either, since by now I'd read the likes of the British *Phantom* magazine as well. Even the married folk had far more in common with fictional couples than any I'd met in life. Yet in retrospect I have the unsettling impression that these jerry-built imitative tales of mine weren't especially inferior to some of the fiction then seeing print, and might even have found a place in, say, *Phantom*.

Much dull stuff burdened that magazine—hack work cranked out by writers with, on the evidence, no love of the field—until it had recourse in its final issues to reprinting tales from *Weird Tales*, raising the tone with Leiber and Wakefield and others. I did submit a poem—well, a bit of verse—only to learn that the magazine was ceasing publication. Might I otherwise have appeared? The world may be thankful for the respite. I doubt my contribution would even have been inadvertently comic, unlike some of *Ghostly Tales* (for instance, the moment where a character consults a dictionary to find out what a shoggoth is, to be solemnly informed that it's a tree with mouths, an image I pinched from "Them Ones", an unauthorised British reprint of Bloch's "Notebook Found in a Deserted House"). At least my book regales us with the spectacle of writerly ambition undermined by inadequate abilities, which can have charms of its own.

Those who know *The Young Visiters* may award the highest prize for charm to Daisy Ashford, but consider her sister Angela, author of *The Jealous Governes* (yes indeed, without doubling the final consonant). I cite just one treasure among many:

> In a few minutes the Dr's bold step was heard at the door and then a loud knock and with a "come in" from Mrs. Hose he entered the room.
>
> "Oh I say Mrs. Hose" he began taking off his hat "I have heard you have been wishing for a baby so I have brought you one and your wish is granted."
>
> "Oh hurrah" said Mrs. Hose "Is it a boy or a girl?"
>
> "Well I don't know" said the Dr. "*quite* but I'll leave you to find out and settle matters" so saying Dr. Pauline took his departure shutting the door with his foot, while he held his precious top hat in his two hands.

We may assume that an eight-year-old Victorian girl might not have been privy to the facts of adult life, but elsewhere special pleading has its limits. I'm looking at myself or at least some early stuff. I wrote but failed to complete a detective novel, *Murder by Moonlight*, when I was fourteen. Its characters are feeble imitations of the kinds of suspects and investigators to be found in the novels of John Dickson Carr, which I was striving to emulate. Other aspects of the book don't have that excuse. I gave one of the investigators a sports car, presumably because his sort drive them in this style of novel. Even if I'd never ridden in one, I was aware it had no roof; that's mentioned in the book. How could I not have grasped that the snowfalls prevalent throughout the narrative might, shall we say, cause a problem? The heroic chap climbs in and drives off, apparently unaware his car is full of snow. Perhaps this betrays no more than a lapse of concentration on the part of the youthful author, but scrutinising the rest of the piece has led me to believe aspects of the book demonstrate the imperfect way he grasped the world.

Of course, or at any rate I hope, it's also fun. Incompetence of this and other sorts was commoner in films, usually independent, than books until self-publication grew rife. Not every self-published book cries out for intensive editing if not euthanasia—Terry Lamsley's first is a splendid exception—but a dispiriting number do. It might be unfair to single any out, and in any case I wouldn't know where to begin. Are films fairer game? Is any movie more inexhaustibly entertaining than *Plan 9 from Outer Space*? Kathleen Coldiron's affectionate Electric Dreamhouse monograph points out details I'd never previously appreciated. Few filmmakers can outdo Ed Wood for creative earnestness coupled with derisory resources, employed with indefatigable enthusiasm and even ramshackle inventiveness. *Plan 9* in particular, and Tim Burton's account of the production, serve as salutary reminders how similar the creative process may be (and certainly feel) for the creator no matter their level of talent. David Thomson warns us enjoying the film could undermine our critical sense, but this hasn't befallen me, and it remains a favourite. I suspect Thomson might prefer to watch it rather than anything directed by Richard Attenborough (as would I). We can only wonder whether, had Wood been around to learn of the reputation he and his work have gathered, he would have said it was always meant to be a laugh, as Tommy Wiseau (*The Room*) and Claudio Fragasso (*Troll 2*) retrospectively claimed of their films. Perhaps some folk may believe them. By contrast, James Nguyen doggedly insists that his *Birdemic: Shock and Terror* is a serious and important work rather than unfailingly hilarious, with effects at least as special as any of Ed Wood's and performances to match. I can't resist appending the blurb from Nguyen's forty-eight-page memoir of making his film, though we can only speculate about the authorship of this paragraph:

BIRDEMIC: The Romantic Thriller That Became a Cult Sensation tells the fascinating and inspiring true story of the new American cult classic BIRDEMIC—Shock and Terror. Told from the personal perspective of the film's visionary creator, Director

James Nguyen who is among the new generation of auteurs in the 21st Century, BIRDEMIC—Shock and Terror became what Nguyen likes to call "a cult sensation hit movie!" Produced for less than $10,000, this meditation on Hitchcock's classic and the environmental chaos caused by the Industrial Age garnered front page coverage from *The New York Times*, in addition to stories broadcast on CBS Morning News, ABC World News With Diane Sawyer and BBC World News. (The tone of the *New York Times* piece can be gauged from lines such as "Crowds in Austin, Tex., Phoenix and Los Angeles have thrilled to its stilted dialogue, substandard production values and young heroes who defend themselves with coat hangers.")

Did prose equivalents of these films ever see professional publication? They did indeed, and I'm disconcerted afresh by the notion that the tales I wrote when eleven were no worse than some of the contemporary work in the field. I'll exempt the products of Badger Books, most of which were written by R. Lionel Fanthorpe in collaboration with his wife Patricia under a bewildering array of pseudonyms, often deriving from his real name. I suspect that Fanthorpe, having learned that the publishers rarely read the material they rushed into print, resolved to have what fun he could while writing each book in a week or less. Just one example—the scene in *Uranium 235* (credited to "John E. Muller") in which "three senior scientists" have a scientific discussion: Evan William Evans utters lines such as "What's the matter, then, look you?" and calls his fellow boffins "dai bach" while Shaughan O'Reilly comments "Ah, bejabbers" and styles his colleagues "me bhoy", in the face of all of which Stuart MacEwan contents himself with saying "Aye" a lot. John Steepens, Joe H. Stennets, Tone J. Phenses and Josh Spentene recently edited a collection of *New Supernatural Tales* by the Fanthorpes for Drugstore Indian Press.

Can I make the same allowances for Digit Books? Quite a few of their titles need none, even once they branched into science fiction: their list was graced by Aldiss, Dickson, Pohl and Kornbluth and others. While their edition of *The Horror from the Hills* shares the bizarre blurb of the Belmont paperback ("This novel was written inside a capsule, travelling through space to a dimension we should hope never to know"), it's credited to Frank Belknap Long. . . . (that is to say, the author's name followed by the ellipsis; what are we to conclude has befallen him?) I wonder if this curious packaging implies the presence of an eccentric editor. Such a person might be thought responsible for purchasing the likes of Nal Rafcam (*The Troglodytes*, famed for such lines as "The echoing of the lesser explosion left the commandos effete") and Terence Haile.

Do I sense a lack of recognition in my readers? Let me present Haile's *Space Train* ("Sabotage Sent Them to the Skies!" says the cover, which does indeed depict a train shooting not merely into space but into the clutches of a colossal robot crab). Our hero, Michael Glyce, is a farmer's son who lives with his mother, who knows that "a fierce flame of determination blazed beneath his shirt". He's building a model train "that would travel between five and ten times as fast as the conventional types" in the back garden. At a dance he meets Alice Demers, daughter of a businessman who wants a swifter means of transport for his tractor parts. "For a farmer," she comments, "you seem very interested in the opposite sex." Glyce succeeds in contacting her father by insisting to "the little girl" (a receptionist) that it's a matter of life and death. Once his frustration bursts "into an explosive verbal cascade" he wins Demers over, and they arrange to meet at a crossroads prior to a demonstration of the train. "I shall be wearing a fawn trilby and green raincoat." We may conclude the author's notions of human behaviour are as fanciful as his attitude to science. "As was his habit when he had 'scored' a success, Mike drew out his pipe and rubbed it against his nose."

Instead of her father, Alice turns up at the rendezvous. "Sending a woman to talk about rocket-engines!" Glyce complains. "The man must be off his head!" In fact she has been sent to postpone the meeting. "A particularly ragged tramp" shows up at the Glyce farm and proves to be Erasmus John Mediu, previously an atomic scientist, who appears to think the atom was invented. Demers watches the train run and, having decided that a full-scale version could travel at three thousand miles an hour on the existing rail network, elects to fund the entire development. When the network turns the notion down, Mrs Glyce arranges for rails to be laid between the flowerbeds in a neighbour's grounds. Apparently cabin pressure ensures her son feels no ill effects at three thousand miles an hour, and the Minister of Transport is sufficiently impressed by the demonstration to adopt the technology for the network.

Alice concludes Glyce befriended her to reach her father and declares she feels "like a piece of sullied cloth removed from a boiled pudding." Laden with dignitaries (not least the entire British Cabinet and leaders of the Opposition), the rocket train flies off the track outside Birmingham and, "looking like an ugly string of sausages", sails into space, where it travels for several days at twenty-five thousand miles an hour. Apart from a little difficulty with breathing, Glyce and his passengers don't seem unduly bothered. He plans to land on the moon and then take off for home, only to find the train has strayed into a web of space crabs big as buses. Having been extravagantly magnified on the cover, they've been waiting in the wings for almost the entire book. They're allotted two pages, where they just have time to emit a hot breath before the train goes into reverse and crash-lands back on Earth. Off it zips to Birmingham, its passengers and drivers uninjured, only to crash into another train. The saboteur is at work again, having gone mad in the common manner of scientists, but apparently crabs stuck on the front of Glyce's train save the day or cause the collision—take your pick, which is more than our author does. At least he accords us and his characters a romantic resolution, perhaps to placate female readers who he imagines won't want to read about space.

I wonder how extreme my claim that I might have been published alongside some, though emphatically not most, of my adult contemporaries may seem now. When I was nine I completed a novella, *Dogs in the Stratosphere*. Though it's lost (and the world may sigh with relief), my memory suggests it wasn't wholly unlike Simak's *City* (then a favourite of mine) retold by Terence Haile (whose work I wouldn't encounter for many years). I return to my opening observation. Some fiction reads like the product of arrested development, and how much truth may it tell about the writer? Perhaps more than the writer would like. Perhaps that should send me to scrutinise my own stuff.

The Scandinavian Abyss

Karen Joan Kohoutek

ANDERS FAGER. *Swedish Cults*. Translated by Ian Lemke and Henning Koch. Richmond, VA: Valancourt Books, 2022. 229 pp. $29.99 hc. ISBN: 9781954321564. $16.99 tpb. ISBN: 9781954321571.

The pantheon of monsters from the work of H. P. Lovecraft has spawned, now, generations of writers who have taken Lovecraft's creations and used them in their own work: a lot of literary takes in recent years. Maybe more than most of us really need! Thankfully, his "Cthulhu Mythos," full of cosmically threatening elder gods, has inspired more than just poor imitations and pastiches—it is also constantly inspiring a wider variety of fiction. A new and critically acclaimed entry in this field, Anders Fager's *Swedish Cults*, explores a world in which Lovecraftian beings exist in a non-Lovecraftian world, contemporary Sweden, described in a decidedly non-Lovecraftian style.

There's no ambiguity about the Lovecraftian nature of these particular Swedish cults, since Fager directly uses the names and attributes of beings out of the Mythos tales. Yog-Sothoth and Carcosa are mentioned by name, as is Ittakva, a.k.a. Ithaqua, who was added to the Mythos by August Derleth. Shub-Niggurath, the Goat with a Thousand Young, stars in one of the stories, and other monsters strip away sanity and reality, or open gateways into a cosmic abyss, which would have made the influence clear even out of this context.

Fager makes no attempt at an updated version of Lovecraft's style, or the atmosphere associated with him. Instead of murky depths, rendered in shadow and suggestion, the language has a sharp, brightly-lit precision. To choose one random example, Lovecraft's famous "The Call of Cthulhu" has a single paragraph containing a "tenebrousness" that "burst forth like smoke from its aeon-long imprisonment, visibly darkening the sun as it slunk away into the shrunken and gibbous sky on flapping membraneous wings," and something that "lumbered slobberingly into sight and gropingly squeezed Its gelatinous green immensity through the black doorway into the tainted outside air of that poison city of madness."

Here, though, everything characteristic of Lovecraft's style has been stripped away: "This isn't a goat. It's a fucking slime monster. Standing two yards from her. Stinking like a garbage dump. So disgusting."

There's some variety, but overall, the sentences are short and fragmented, leading to a fast pace and forward momentum that can have its own beauty; for example: "A road of silver. Thousands of years old. The road from the dance pavilion to the grove by the bog. The bog where the tree branches look like slowly swaying octopus tentacles." But it can also become a little exhausting.

So in the lengthy road-trip story "Grandma's Journey," I could appreciate the way Fager piles up detail to ground its narrative of supernatural beings and cosmic forces in the most everyday experiences: all the stages of the journey, with the driving, the gas station stops, snacks and cigarettes, in addition to more dramatic incidents along the way. At the same time, there was a lot of sameness in its short, often clinical sentences, and I thought I was going to go mad myself if I read the sentence "Grandma is going on a journey" one more time. Some stylistic choices, like that kind of repetition, are just going to be more effective for some people than others.

In all the accumulated detail, there are generally no cues about the author's attitude or intentions, or what he expects the readers to feel. That objectivity, or at least the veneer of objectivity, seems common to a lot of contemporary writing, and unfortunately it can leave me cold. For example, "In the Osterholm" shows the willingness of a young couple to be seduced by evil for economic gain and status. As the situation grows ever uglier for the social climbers, I wondered if it's a vivid picture of human psychology, or is it is a case of classist mockery?

Personally, I found myself more invested when there were actual points of view on display, even in the form of debate between varied characters. The ideas coming out of this give a sense of where to position ourselves, and tease out some larger themes. An example of this is in "Miss Witt's Great Work," when the title character argues at a social gathering that the only modern painter most people can name is the long-dead Picasso. In a work with so many overt references to Lovecraft's work, and the larger Mythos that has developed around it, I wondered if this was a commentary on the continued preeminence of Lovecraft in weird circles, and the need for something new. I can't tell from the text if I'm onto something, but it's something to think about.

This English translation is the work of Ian Lemke and Henning Koch and comes from Valancourt Press, which is—full disclosure—my favorite publisher. I've bought countless Gothic and Victorian novels from them, although they have branched out into the literature of the 20th and 21st centuries, and this publication fits in with their focus on contemporary horror literature in translation.

There Are More Things

The joey Zone

ARS NECRONOMICA 2022. *The Visual Divine of the Dark Cosmos, Here and Beyond*. Providence, RI: AS220 Aborn Gallery. August 11–28, 2022.

The biennial art exhibition Ars Necronomica is both an independent entity and part of a continuing tradition begun in 2013 with the regeneration of NecronomiCon [Providence]. H. P. Lovecraft, along with the "Lovecraft Circle" of related authors (for example, Robert E. Howard and Clark Ashton Smith) has rightly "been acknowledged as the godfather to collaborative creative culture . . . in this tradition of collaboration" the art show sets out to *"honor the legacy and life of a literary iconoclast."* These words, with this reviewer's added emphasis, come from the 2013 exhibition's Mission Statement. The convention's 2017 Memento Book defined this further: "Each installment of the exhibition is a chapter in a larger story—our curatorial perception of not just a Lovecraftian aesthetic but how we see weird art itself."

This year's fifth perception was held in conjunction with the convention itself now looking beyond H. P. Lovecraft "to all the latest authors and artists who are now expanding the field of [the Weird]" with admission that many of them now don't draw "any influence from Lovecraft" (*MOTIF* magazine, August 3, 2022). Only nineteen of the fifty pieces in the exhibit were Lovecraftian, displaying perhaps, say, a similar tentacular physiognomy, if not a direct representation, inherent in some of Lovecraft's fictitious taxonomies. Of the remaining number were, however, several deserving wall space in any showcase, of Weird or otherwise.

Abomination takes many forms.

Foremost among these was Alan Brown's watercolor with gouache entitled "Magic Moves," boasting a hand carved figural frame and colour juxtaposition that itself appeared to render line in three dimensions. A depiction of Grendel (from *Beowulf*) as The Hanged Man of Tarot (also a grim leitmotif in William Lindsay Gresham's *Nightmare Alley*), it was a welcome return of this artist's work to Ars Necronomica after his last entry in 2017. Brown bears credit for much of the better art on successful early pressings by Cadabra Records, starting with *The Hound* and especially *The Lurking Fear*, with a member of the Martense clan perfectly defined for that LP's inner gatefold sleeve.

Kings in darkness: Maegan Lemay's "The Abyss."

Rhode Island inkslinger Maegan Lemay was clearly the breakout star of this year's convention. Designing Necronomi-Con's official t-shirt (which was rumored to have sold out by Saturday of the schedule), she was also responsible for the poster of one of the musical concerts held as part of the festivities. The band Cirith Ungol—despite their Tolkien derived moniker—has also used Michael Moorcock's Elric on their record covers and Maegan depicted the albino Melnibonean and Stormbringer handily with her strong sword, er—tattooing arm. Lemay's style displays skill similarly found in the work of, say, Brian Bolland or even Virgil Finlay, this being evident in her submission to Ars Necronomica, "The Abyss."

Notable other pieces on display included that by Nick Gucker; a darker than usual painting by one of the exhibition's co-curators, Jennifer Hrabota Lesser, "Where the Black Stars Rise;" Matt Jaffe's original for John Langan's collection *Children of the Fang*; and two works by the sadly recently deceased Marcello Gallegos.

In order to truly see a thing, one must first understand it.

More Mythos than these was the art of Liv Rainey Smith, a printmaker from Portland, Oregon, without whom Ars Necronomica would not be the quality show that it has been throughout the years. A true xylographiliac, she carves out bold lines that delineate true knowledge of The Arcane. "Through the Gates" revisits a deity Smith had summoned for the 2013 exhibition, the great subterranean toad god, Tsathoggua. Liv's imprint on our scene is worthy of many editions—A geas then upon her that they have an eternal run!

Originals of other published work on display included Jason Eckhardt's scratchboard of "The Alert" (*The New Annotated H. P. Lovecraft*) and Josh Yelle's triptych for the Robert H. Waugh collections put out by the publisher of this journal. Sculptors contributed more of the Lovecraftian based art, from Karen Main's circular polymer clay leering entity "GYACK," to Gage Prentiss' "Lake Expedition Fossil Specimen #44." a crinoidian inhabitant monstrous in size, to exhibition versions of molds by stalwarts Jason McKittrick and Joe

Liv Rainey Smith gives sacrifice to a Hellmouth under Hyperborea in "Through The Gates."

Broers. One is in constant awe of all those working in this medium, making the indescribable tangible.

From what secret regions of astronomy or time, from what ancient and now incalculable twilight . . . it reached this South American suburb . . .

From the boulevards of Buenos Aires, the home of Borges–from whom these quotes are taken–we were honored to welcome as this year's Artist Guest of Honor Santiago Caruso. His oeuvre epitomizes the legacy and future of what should be Ars Necronomica. Caruso has illuminated the writings of Dante, Kafka, Schwob and Lautréamont, his paintings for *Los cantos de Maldoror* (2016) being the standout ("Among the best I've seen," wrote 2015 Artist Guest of Honor John Coulthart). Con attendees may know Santiago better from editions of Chambers, Bierce, Campbell or Pugmire including his art. For this exhibition, however, eleven watercolors were torn or razored (then fortunately framed) from a 2022 notebook—all of them illustrating the work of H. P. Lovecraft.

In 2015, Ars Necronomica had shown a handful of Caruso's work, some done in monochromatic scratchboard. His current medium glowed with colours giving additional sustenance to sentient miasmas emanating from below ("The Unnameable Cemetery") or within ("The Witch House"—also used as the cover of this year's Memento Book—it's gambreled structure seemingly high lit ala director Richard Stanley). This reviewer's favorite selection was "'Til The Kingsport Cathedral" based on Lovecraft's "The Festival." The rolling sea and dark universe yawn upon another high house in the mist "gleaming out in the cold dusk" extending a spir'd finger towards "Orion and the archaic stars." It *is* the Yuletide.

Yet more groundbreaking was another work illustrating "The Dreams in the Witch House." Due to its deep incarnadined hues, it is difficult for even the finest photogravure to grant justice in reproduction to what was seen *in persona*: An *accurate* pictorial depiction of "the alien curves and spirals of some ethereal vortex" obeying "laws unknown to the physics and mathematics of any conceivable cosmos." Santiago has accomplished no mean feat of taking us—to use the title of Fritz Leiber's famous essay—*through hyperspace with Brown Jenkin*. This visual divination, along with his other ten offerings, have alone raised the bar on Lovecraftian as well as Weird art in general, going on from here into the beyond. A fuller (?) exhibition promised in 2024 may be possible, but no finer art can be perceived in our philosophy. We will not flinch in the hope of being proved wrong.

Matt Jaffe channels Jeffrey Catherine Jones in "Children of The Fang." (Photo courtesy of Michelle Souliere.)

Curiosity got the better of fear, and I did not close my eyes.

*Artist Guest of Honor Santiago Caruso's early work
used for Claudio Garcia Fanlo's* Profundo Buenos Aires
transformed for The Divine City.

NecronomiCon Providence:
It Isn't Just the Money

As reported by Darrell Schweitzer

In the *Star Trek* universe it would be described in terms of *Ferengi orgasms*, which is that ecstatic rush experienced by those big-eared, money-grubbing aliens when someone hands them a large amount of *latinum*, er, I mean currency, and then someone else does, and someone else does. Since I went to NecronomiCon Providence as a vendor, my experience may have been a bit more limited than some. Lovecraftians *do* spend money like water if you've got the right stuff, and sales are absolutely amazing, orders of magnitude beyond any other convention, even conventions equally as large, such as a World Science Fiction Convention. I wear a button which features another non-Lovecraftian reference—it says PURCHASE MASS QUANTITIES—and indeed the customers do. The typical purchase is a stack of books, my own titles, both Wildside trade paperbacks and my Fedogan & Bremer collection, *Awaiting Strange Gods,* plus my PS Publishing Lovecraftian anthologies. Most of the action seemed to be in the front row of the table, the F&G book (I went through a whole crate of them) and the PS titles. I sold a Don Grant first edition of Robert E. Howard's *The Gent from Bear Creek* for a hundred dollars within an hour of opening.

All those $35 hardcovers and $15 trade paperbacks do add up.

It's a veritable orgy of greed, or perhaps more nobly, a major exercise in spreading my own literary effusions out into the world at a rate better than the publishers can do. But I want to emphasize that this is not a sales report.

The really good thing about NecronomiCon Providence this year is that it happened at all. After the onset of the Plague, the world was not the same. NecronomiCon should have been last year. It used to be on odd-numbered years, but in 2021 it was a casualty of the pandemic. So it was a great relief to see the convention back from the dead, very much in its familiar form. I think the attendance was a little lower than usual, but it was certainly in the low thousands. It felt like a homecoming, a return to tradition, a time of Festival older than Memphis and mankind, as the stars were right and the eldritch folk gathered and one saw old friends and met new ones.

The one concession to COVID-19 was that mask policies were strictly enforced. Once, in the dealers' room, my mask had slipped down to my chin, and even though I was well away from anyone behind my table, a minion immediately asked me to put it on properly. As well he should have. We even wore masks while speaking on panels. That being the case, I thought I should at least wear interesting masks, and so came equipped with one with Cthulhuoid tentacles, and, just to be iconoclastic, another that features the Three Stooges. (But isn't Curly an avatar of the Crawling Chaos, Nyarlathotep . . .?) At the Prayer Breakfast Sunday morning, for once hymn lyrics were *not* provided to the general congregation, lest everybody singing at once turn it into a super-spreader event. (If this seems quaint in some parts of America, I can only say that Yankees seem to have more respect for public health measures than some folks elsewhere.) We also lost our organist due to coronavirus concerns, and so croaked and cackled *a capella*. As choir leader, I urged the choir to be *loud*. We too were wearing masks.

So, good times. I somehow never laid eyes on any of the guests of honor other than Gemma Files, who said hello briefly. As a vendor I always miss the opening ceremonies, because I am setting up then, and have as yet never been inside the First Baptist Church, a.k.a. the Yes We Have No Bananas Church. I also managed to miss the art reception Thursday evening, because I hadn't looked at my pocket program closely enough in the rush to set up, register, etc. and didn't know about it, but I did go to the outdoor street party, where there was music and eldritch musicians in spectacularly cosmic and inhuman costumes. I did in the course of the weekend catch up with Martin Andersson, Peter Cannon, Donovan Loucks, Sean Branney, Will Murray, Derrick Hussey, and many more.

I was on two panels, one about the concept of "Inherited Guilt in Lovecraft," which was particularly highlighted by one of the panelists, Melissa Stewart, who was well prepared to talk about eugenics in Lovecraft's time and how such beliefs influenced not just his fiction, but the whole culture. It seemed to me that the ultimate Lovecraftian story of guilty inheritance must be "Arthur Jermyn." "The original Mrs. Jermyn," I suggested, "must have been an ape of singular charm." I also gave a reading, and was on another panel about "What Have We Lost?" I suggested that in a field of such obsessive collectors as our own we have lost very little in the sense of physical copies of anything other than hectographed fanzines, but what we have lost is *voices*. We can no longer actually talk to the giants who once walked the Earth and knew Lovecraft and his colleagues. There was a time when you could come to one of these conventions and meet Frank Belknap Long, Manly Wade Wellman, H. Warner Munn, Sprague de Camp, and many more who are no longer with us. Not long before this year's convention we lost former NecronomiCon guest of honor Richard Lupoff.

The rest of the programming, as far as I could tell, was really excellent, striking a good balance between antiquarianism and modern interests. I did get to as many performances as I could, managing to take in Robert Lloyd Parry's brilliant interpretation of M. R. James's "Count Magnus" and one of the Lovecraft Historical Society's radio plays, this time, "The Horror in the Museum." It was a very busy, rushed weekend. The one dead time for me was about 2 hours Saturday night during the Eldritch Ball (I am not much of a dancer), but I used this to be interviewed at length by Christopher Nightingale, an Englishman who is working on what will likely be a first-rate documentary about Lord Dunsany.

This was one of those conventions where you wish you could be several places at once. I spent most of the days selling books and meeting readers. At NecronomiCons I am, I guess I can say honestly, something of a celebrity, or at least more than a mere fixture. I really do meet people who have read and enjoyed my work and want more. (Then the cash starts flowing again . . .) The Sunday morning Cthulhu Prayer Breakfast, as mentioned above, was another highlight, as always. Brothers Cody Goodfellow and Anthony Teth preached. I quite literally sang for my breakfast. If some of us were in our own original key and time, well, the Innsmouth Tabernacle Choir can only be expected resonate cosmic chaos and madness a little bit.

A shambling good time was had by all. I made a point of thanking the chairman, Niels Hobbs, for causing this to happen.

One serious note I will add, relating to my vending experience: I was doing very well. Hippocampus Press was doing well. Necronomicon Press was there. The HPL Historical Society was there with a variety of products. There were other independent book publishers present, a t-shirt vendor, people selling art, eldritch idols, gaming materials, and the like; but other than one guy with some overpriced science fiction paperbacks (who did not seem to be doing well), I did not see much in the way of antiquarian books there. This is a niche that is still open. Some enterprising book dealer with a good and reasonably priced stock of old volumes of Dunsany, Machen, Blackwood, M. R. James, *Weird Tales* and other magazines of interest, classic ghost story anthologies, and the like could really clean up at NecronomiCon. So I hope that in the future somebody will.

Hunter's Moon Homecoming

CM Schneider

There's somethin' about small town festivals, you know? They always bring out everybody. Even the folks you didn't know existed or thought died, or kids in college. There's nothing quite like it.

I grew up in Feuville and we do somethin' special. Somethin' unique. I never thought of it as weird, but I guess no one else thinks theirs is either. They all just growed up with their county fairs and zombie walks, and we had ours.

Did you know there's places that still got Harvest Moon festivals? We in Feuville don't. Nothing that silly. But they do. They do and what's more, they do 'em late. Late enough to be into October and still they calls 'em harvest festivals. Anyone who's lived in a farm town'll tell you that that ain't right. Harvest is in September. October is hunting season, We have a Hunter's Moon festival.

Anyways, small town festivals are special. They bring out all kinds. I remember I drove through the night to visit Feuville's my first year in college, which probably weren't a great idea on those roads but I was younger then. More naive.

I pulled up to the little whitish farmhouse around dawn. Parked next to Ma's battered ol' Chevy and looked at the fog for a few minutes. Fog always makes me think of ghosts. I know October's pumpkin season in the city, but out here, it's creepy in the early mornin'. Not that I believed in ghosts or nothin'. Just always seemed real in the fog, like a natural habitat.

Ma was already up when I walked in. She gave me a big hug like moms do, all smiles.

"Clare, hun. You made it," she said and, "How was school?"

All college kids have bad days and I didn't wanna tell her that I'd found the bottle. I'd avoided it like a sin in high school, which felt like so long ago, but I guess was only six months. Seemed longer.

"School's good," I said and asked about coffee.

"I'll make some. Want some pancakes, hun?"

"Sure. I'mma try to nap first."

She nodded and I went down the hall to my old room. I didn't sleep. There was a staleness to the familiarity. Like the room needed airing out or the ceiling was drooping just a bit more than I remembered. My video game posters still hung on the wall, straight in their frames. I know most folks don't bother with posters, but I like 'em. They're artistic and not in the way some granny might make with shaky hands an' try to sell to tourists. They're skillful.

That's about when Shep, our aged pit bull, jumped me. I didn't know he could still jump. Must've missed me. He's big and I had to push him off. Giving me that sad kind of look that an old, tired dog gives when his feelings're hurt, so I scritched his ears. He always liked that. We just laid there for a bit, me scritchin' his head and his chin on my chest.

Pancakes start smellin' in the kitchen. Bacon too. And Shep decided it were time for breakfast. Ma was probly waitin' for us.

We had coffee and she gossiped and asked if I'd heard about the Groyen boy. I hadn't, thinking maybe he'd died and gotten out of his misery.

"He got that surgery they was praying for. Just last month," Ma said. "Finally old enough. The doc said he had grown into all his parts and just needed to complete the package. Itn't funny, hun?"

"That's great, Ma."

"His whole arm's new."

Now, I don't like to talk bad about folks, mind. But I don't like fake arms an' legs neither. I found that out in Mr. Sanchez's bio class in high school. He was telling us how the batteries and nerves worked together, and I went an' vomited all over my desk. I don't think they's gross or anything. Just makes me queasy is all.

Ma forgot that, I thought. She forgot a lot, but so did I.

"It uses the smallest little batteries you ever seen, hun. Hun? You listenin'?"

I nodded.

"How's school, hun?"

"Still fine," I said.

It's a strange thing, comin' home from the big city. Things seem different. I remember that Ma died when I came home late after my junior prom, but here she is, doing the same things she always did. I just can't see her the same way, knowin' she died.

But part of me knows that's not how the world works. It's funny, ain't it? The world works different in the city. Here, in the country, in these small southern towns city folks call the Bible Belt, the world just works different.

I took a bite of my pancakes. I can still remember the taste of the canned pumpkin pie in 'em. Ma always made 'em that way, but never wrote down the recipe so I can't make 'em without her. I think she adds somethin' when I'm not looking.

"You come home for the fest?" she asked.

I nod.

"You get a costume?"

I nod again, still chewing.

"Well, hun?"

I grinned and swallowed. "It's in the car."

"How'd you choose it?"

"The app."

She blinked. "What app?"

"Oh, you know, Ma, our app." It was my ticket to college, got a full ride scholarship. See, entrepreneurship is a big deal in farmtown schools and we had a competition every year in high school. I partnered with a couple kids who was good with computers and we made Imagyn. You'd load in your body scan and the app scanned your clothes tags to show you what you'd look like in your clothes. We even had a deal with some of the mall clothing stores so folks could use their catalog an' order direct from the store. It was like a game, but practical. Well, practical for city livin'. Out here, we mostly just wear jeans and whatever t-shirt suits the occasion.

"Right, your app." She looked at the table. Grampa made it outta some old barn wood after the war.

"It's okay, Ma," I told her, and it weren't a lie. Not really. She forgot things sometimes.

Ma shrugs. "It's the last year you'll be able to go costumed."

I nodded. I'd be twenty next year. Too old to dress up for

the festival, because I'd be an adult. I'd be expected to be married soon too. And give my man kids. I wouldn't work much after that. Makes me wonder, sometimes, why I bother with school. It's this town, I guess. Nothing changes. It felt like a trap, everybody trapped together. Destiny. As people, we're born, we grow, we work hard just to eke out a little bit extra, and we die. Sometimes, I lie awake, worryin' all I'll ever be is a baby factory for a farmer. Don't need any education for that.

It still scares the fuck out of me.

Ma left me at the table to finish my pancakes while she went to get ready.

It's funny. This place makes me think of that night. The night she died. It wasn't a bad night, I guess, but my prom didn't go as intended. I s'pose that's true for most girls.

"I'm just putting my face on!" Ma yelled from the bathroom.

I remember now that she's somethin' else. I don't know how I could forget it, but I always do. My thoughts always got circular about this, tryin' to remember longer, make it stick. Ma died a year and half ago. I guess that's why I moved out early, as soon as I could.

"I'm gonna shower!" I yell back.

The shower felt good. Hot and earthy, tasting of the well out back. I didn't want to think about Ma, about the fact that she's not human. She's just not. She can't be. I mean, she's like Ma was, but Ma died. There weren't no funeral or anything, weren't no body. She run off into the night and this Ma came back.

I grab the soapbar. It's slick with the salty water, the softener's acting up again. I wait for the water to clear up before rinsing so I don't get itchy later. I can't stand itchiness. Makes me think of the old skinwalker stories Pa used to tell back when his cancer got bad.

'I feel like the dark lady,' he'd say, the cancer flakin' his skin, then getting into his blood and bones. He died when I was ten.

Ma was loadin' the truck with several cakes and pies when I got out. Say what you will about Ma, but, dead or alive, no one made a better cake in this county.

I helped her load the last of the baked goods and my

mouth watered while staring at her spiced carrot cake. It was always my favorite. I could smell the rum before I even got near it and it was sure temptin' to hide it for myself, but I knew I'd never get away with it.

Once everthin' was loaded, we headed to town. There's a sort of historic district, but the reality is the town just never knocked down the old buildings. The town square might as well have been a public museum to the town's history since its founding, more or less kept functional. Old brick and mortar type buildings with their expensive looking facades from a century ago.

The Hunter's Moon festival takes place in the park on the square. It used to be the First Baptist Church, but lightning had burned it down and folks just let the oak trees grow back and built the Second Baptist Church a few blocks away.

The carnival was already set up. There was an empty lot on the square and the ferris wheel peeked up between the old two-story buildings. Workers, who looked more like Walmart employees than carnies, wandered, bottles in hand. One of them waved and I saw he was Jimmy. I waved back and he jogged over. I felt like grimacing.

Jimmy was a football star in high school. Yeah, I know how typical that sounds. But we went to state all three years he was fullback. He'd only gotten bigger. He was over six foot and had that well-fed look. The kind of figure where you can't tell if a guy's overweight or muscled unless he takes his shirt off. I hoped he wouldn't though. I'm not that kind of girl.

"Clare!" He acted like he was gonna give me a hug, but paused. I hugged him anyway. It's hot out and even though I showered, I know I was startin' to smell. A little more wouldn't hurt anything.

"It's been awhile," he said.

"Yeah, I went off to school."

"And I quit early."

I weren't real sure what to say to that. Jimmy and me, we used to be good friends. Stuff got weird between us when he asked me to prom and I turned him down. He quit school after junior year and I hadn't ever seen him happier. He still had the biggest smile. It's not toothy or nothing, just big.

"Well, you're back for the fest?"

I nodded. Funny, I never thought I did a lot of that. Guess I do. Maybe that's on the town too.

"It'll be a treat. I getta work the bar." He winked, 'cause everybody knowed his family's a bunch of drunks and he weren't no better. "I'm the bouncer."

"Is that legal?" I asked. He was, well, he must've been only twenty.

"Yup." He was proud of it. "I can't drink it and they won't let me serve it, even though you can at eighteen, but I can keep folks in line."

"You'll do good," I said.

He nodded, "Will you be around?"

"Yeah, I'll be around."

"Nah, I mean, will you come by the bar tonight?"

"I can't drink."

"Nah, nah, but we'll have dancin'." He looked so hopeful.

"I'll see. I'm hoping to spend time with Emma Lee."

"Jones?"

"Heusenfeld."

He nodded. "I don't think she's back from school."

I shrugged. I hadn't seen Emma Lee since she moved away last year.

"Maybe she's late," I said.

"Maybe."

There was a weird silence. I was waiting for him to say somethin' but he just looked at me. Ma waved at me from the car, probably hoping Jimmy would help us unload everythin' even though she already had a gaggle of highschool kids helpin' her.

"Well, I need to help Ma," I said.

"Yeah, I gotta get back to setting up. No breaks 'til we're done. Good seein' ya, Clare."

"You too." I watched him go. He seemed different than he did in school. I think he walked slow. Maybe he was tired? Now I think of it, everythin' in town seemed tired looking.

I grabbed the last cake and followed Ma into the park. The big old oaks swayed in the breeze and there were a few folks chatting around the tables. One of them had two big water coolers, one orange, one yellow, probably sweet tea and lemonade, where Miz Heusenfeld had set up drinks. Miz Jones headed toward Ma with a glass. Several boys helped with the carrying. I reckon a pie went missing, but couldn't say by who.

Miz Jones handed Ma her glass and asked if I wanted anything.

What I wanted was a beer, but I said, "Lemonade's fine."

She smiled and walked to the drink table, the one with the colored coolers. The heat's never as bad under the trees, but my shirt clung to my skin like I'd been running. I looked around and saw Miz Heusenfeld talking to Mr. Groyen. They were both teachers and I could hear they were talking about work when I walked up.

"Oh, Clare, dear," Miz Heusenfeld said. "I didn't know you were back."

"I drove in last night. Is Emma Lee coming? I haven't seen her around."

"No, she's working at a club in the city, bless her heart. She never has weekends off."

"Oh," I said, "good for her." I wish I meant it. Miz Heusenfeld looked like your average small town woman. She's heavier than Ma, but not much. Her hair was dyed streaky blonde, like the stylist went overboard trying to do highlights.

Mr. Groyen is a small man and stoops. He reminded me of Ma. They both moved the same way, slow and kinda unsteady, but with strength underneath, like willpower is all they need.

He smiled weakly at me. "Clare, how's the coast?"

"Hot," I said. "I got a lot more sun than I expected."

"Well, you tan nicely."

I blushed, embarrassed. Mr. Groyen was probably the sweetest man I've ever met. He could compliment you and seein' it on paper, you'd swear he was a perv flirting with a gal. He weren't though. He was more like a doctor describing how an organ works, but he meant to be nice. Folks sometimes talked about his wife, wondering why she left him and the boy and disappeared, but never when he was around.

"A pity young Emma Lee can't come."

"Yeah."

"I was hoping to get her help with something." He looked at me kinda earnest.

"What was that?"

"Well," he leaned in, and Miz Heusenfeld and me, we did too. "You know how the Hunt goes. Gotta wrangle the teens and scare them so they don't find the cake."

"And you want me to help you with the monsters?"

"Well, I was going to ask Emma Lee, but if you're interested, I could use the help." He whispered, "Your mother made the cake this year."

"I'll help."

He smiled at me.

"Do I hafta wear a costume?"

"Only a mask."

"Thank you, Clare. I'm gettin' too old for runnin' around the woods," Miz Heusenfeld said.

"The nature trail could use a clean up," Mr. Groyen said. "A pity we didn't have a chance to do it this year."

"If we catch all the kids, we get the cake?" I asked.

"Mmm? Ah, I suppose so. Hasn't happened before."

I smiled at him. "Could happen this year."

"Meet me behind the church an hour after sundown. That should be the right time."

"Thank you again, Clare. See you at church," Miz Heusenfeld said.

"Yes ma'am," I said and left them alone. Miz Jones was chatting with Ma still. A styrofoam cup of neon lemonade was on the table next to them. I picked it up and drank it. It was sweet, maybe too sweet, made from a store-bought mix. But it was cold. It was easily ninety degrees out and I'd stopped sweating. Anyone can tell you that ain't good.

I got a second glass of lemonade from the yellow cooler and went to find somewhere to sit. I settled on a root under one of the biggest trees. The roots around these trees are smooth from kids playin' on them over years. There's not much bite to that bark and it makes a comfortable seat.

I watched the folks around me work. They finished setting up the carnival. I saw Mr. Groyen carry a bag to the church. More lemonade and tea were brought out when the coolers emptied.

Somethin' knocked the cup out of my hand. I screamed. Yeah, I screamed. It's embarrassing, but whatever, everyone saw it.

I was covered in lemonade, I was hot and cold and wet and I looked down and I seen this shoe on my cup. Just a shoe. I think it was blue or grey. Definitely a guy's shoe. Just layin' next to the dirty styrofoam.

I looked up and I saw the Groyen boy with this big O face.

"Sorry," he said.

I glared. It's not right, I know that, but yeah, I glared and yelled at him to get down. He did, shamefaced and slow. I didn't think he could climb trees with only one arm.

"What the hell are you doing in a tree?" I said when he was down and standing there with one shoe on and t'other in the mud.

He shrugged. "That's what boys are supposed to do, right?"

That's when I remembered the prosthetic. Well, saw the prosthetic. It's funny, you know, prosthetics ain't like they used to be. Now they don't just move, they feel. It's like havin' a real arm. I s'pose it is a real arm, just metal. I know it's not somethin' folks choose, having only one arm, but I can't help it making me feel sick seein' it.

I was flushed. I wasn't angry anymore, but I wasn't blushing either. Just emotional, you know?

"You've never climbed a tree?" I couldn't look away from the prosthetic. I barely saw him shake his head.

He shook his head. "I've never been able to." He waved his new arm. It was bigger'n his other arm. A man's arm stuck onto a boy little more'n a kid. "It feels different."

"Different how?" I was feelin' queasy, but was too embarrassed to not make conversation. Gotta be polite, after all.

"I dunno," he said. "Like Pinnochio, I guess. It feels things different is all."

"Huh," I said. I didn't know what else to say. I was feeling pretty . . . Well it sounds bad, but I was feeling exposed, vulnerable. Like a hawk was goin' to swoop down and snatch me for dinner.

"You might wanna clean up," he told me. "Sorry again. I still can't quite tie my shoes right."

"Yeah, fine. It's no big deal." I left him to clean the mess his shoe made. Maybe Pinnochio'll enjoy that feeling.

I got the keys from Ma and went to the truck to change into my costume. I'd changed in the truck before, but never parked in the middle of town. I kept a careful eye out for other people, but no one came around.

I stepped out and examined myself in the door. I don't really look the part, my skin's too light to do a proper Alana Gomez, Lady Adventurer, but I'm the right build and my face ain't too far off. If I'd worn that to college parties, I'd get a lot of comments about the whip. Still would, probably, just different kind of comments.

The torn khakis and black tank-top are warm from the sunlight on the backseat. I reckoned wearin' the jacket was a bad choice, so I carried it. I'd probably want it in the woods tonight. If not for the cold, then for the spiders.

Folks were gathering in the park when I arrived. Kids running around, laughing, whispering. There was popcorn and cotton candy in the air. And a ton of noise. I hadn't realized how quiet it was before. The town was coming alive for the festival. Really alive.

A kid laughed behind me. I felt my mood sour. Why? Because I was upset about the lemonade incident. I know that now. But back then I was just upset.

Anyway, the kids ran past and kicked up dust behind their gallumphin' asses. I watched 'em and saw Jimmy beyond. He waved them into a octagonal pit, not workin', just trying to be helpful.

"*Gagaball's come this far?*" I thought. It was a fun game, but I'd first seen it at college. Hell, it'd only been two months. I had no idea that these little kids could've played. It's a rough game.

Jimmy saw me and waved.

I smiled and waved back.

Someone whistled behind me.

I turned around. The Groyen boy again. He'd got a couple friends with him and he was blushing hard. The other boys looked like punks. Not real punks though. Just the kind of hard looks and dirty mouths teens get out here when they've got a reputation for being trouble.

"Lady, if I'd known you had them clothes, I'd've thrown drinks on you an hour ago," one of the brats said.

"You could use a whippin'," I said.

The other boys whooped and the Groyen boy stared at his feet.

I blushed too, realizin' what I said. One of those stupid things that show up on bad memes.

"Get, assholes!" I about yelled and they hied off. All but the Groyen boy.

"I'm real sorry," he said.

"You too." I watched him leave. He looked like a dog with its tail between its legs running after his friends. I saw Jimmy nod to me and go back to wranglin' kids. I walked over. Last thing I wanted was to be alone right then and Jimmy, despite himself, knew better than to say stupid stuff like that.

That's where Ma found me. Jimmy had convinced me to jump into the pit. I had a good run but got hit by a kid knee-high when she got there.

"Been lookin' for ya, hun," she said.

I shrugged. "Here I am."

I loved Ma, maybe I still do, but she weren't the same person. Not since she died. She used to get this look like she needed the bathroom whenever she had somethin' she wanted to talk about. Now, she just blindsides you with it.

We got somethin' to eat. Turkey legs and funnel cake, I think. What elsc could it be? We was at the festival and neither of us liked deep fried things what shouldn't be.

"Hun?" she asked when we'd eaten a bit. The sun was setting behind us.

"Yeah?"

"Why d'you like that explorer character so much?"

I shrugged. I couldn't explain the relief I felt seeing Alana for the first time. I can't really explain it now. She was smart, strong and didn't really fit in a box. Everythin' I wasn't, but maybe I could be. Potential I guess. Everythin' this town don't have for girls like me.

"I mean, hun, she's a bit of a slut, ain't she?"

My head shot up so fast I felt my neck pop. "There's no sex in the movies, Ma."

"Well," she shrugged, "you know."

I felt more awkward than explaining why I'd been home late from prom. That felt like somethin' that just happens to people, but this was more personal somehow.

"No, Ma, I don't know. What're you tryin' to say? That I'm a slut just because I look up to a woman who's not a good little housewife?"

"No, hun!" The horror on her face made me flush. I shouldn't've gotten mad.

"I just mean, there's better–Oh, what's the word? Like heroes?"

"Role models?"

"Role models, that's it." She smiled.

"You sound like a preacher on youth night."

"Maybe the preacher's got a point."

"Yeah, it's hard to get girls to submit in a society that wants 'em to be equal to men."

Her face hardened. Ma didn't like talk of society changing. Sometimes I wonder if it ever will.

"Look, Ma, I know you mean well," I held her hand. "I just don't think you understand what I want. That's all."

Her mouth twitched, but there was tears in her eyes. "How long you been wanting to say that, hun?"

"A while," I admitted.

We're silent for a while after that. Neither of us wanted to eat anymore and the sound of folks chatting around was a welcomed distraction. I stood after what felt like awkward hours and gathered our trash. The trash cans weren't far away.

Ma was gone when I turned around. She usually disappeared from the festival. I always had friends around to keep me from noticing, I guess. Some of 'em thought she must've been one of the monsters.

The dust was gettin' thicker. The light danced all 'round from the games and rides. Smells of barbeque and popcorn and deep fried everything; meat and cookies and ice cream; chocolate and pickles and funnel cake. Thicker than the dust was the sour smell of cheap beer. Some parts of festivals are all alike.

I wandered around for a bit, waitin' for dark, not wanting to ride any rides. Festivals aren't real festive without friends, you know? Emma Lee was working. Jimmy too now. Maybe Ma had soured my mood. I don't know. I could've gone to see Jimmy. Don't know why I didn't. He was always sweet on me, but I didn't want the attention I guess.

I eventually found my way to the nature trail where the hunt would start. The trail was dark and unlit so the hunters could have a challenge. Miracle no one ever got hurt. The temperature was dropping so I put my jacket on. Pa's old jacket. I don't think Ma noticed, or cared. It still smelled like him, at least how I remember him in those final days. The moon was rising, big and orange enough to blot out the stars. The Hunter's Moon. That's why we were all here tonight, wasn't it? That big ball of rock without life or light of its own?

I saw someone else in the clearing. The Groyen boy was sittin' near the path, starin' at the clearing. I walked over. I'm still not sure why.

"Hey," I said.

He looked at me, nodded and turned back to the clearing.

"Where're your friends?"

"Not here. And they're not my friends."

"Then what're you doin' here?"

"Shhh," he pointed to the clearing. "If you're too loud, they'll hear you and won't come."

Now, I know the story as much as anyone else. The local ghost story, I guess. On a full moon, spirits dance on the ashes of the burned church. Some say they burned it down, 'cause that was their place first. But I never seen anyone who actually believed it so I laughed.

He glared at me.

"What?" he hissed.

"They're not real. . . . Ummm?"

"Ummm?"

"I don't know your name."

"Will. Name's Will. And yeah, they are. I saw them last year. They only come out on the Hunter's Moon."

"That's not true," I thought, but I remembered flashes of darkness on prom night.

We watched the clearing as the moonlight turned to yellow, then white. There was a shimmer between the shadows and moonbeams. I thought I saw somethin' dark move, like a shadow where there wasn't any. I peered at it, but it was nothing. No spirits.

Will sighed, "Not this time." He stood.

"Why're you looking for them?"

"No reason."

"But you've got a reason."

"And I don't wanna share it." He shrugged. "Come on. I've gotta help my dad with his hunt."

"This about your ma?"

He paused, then left. He seemed larger, not like a sixteen year old boy.

I followed him. I had to help his pa too and it was past that time. Now, I wasn't too eager. I'd agreed out of boredom. But if the old spirits're out in these woods, maybe I shouldn't've. Not that I believe in them. It's just easier to think they're fake durin' the day.

His pa was waitin' for us. He nearly danced when he saw us. "Come on, come on. The hunt is about to start!"

Several masks were in a box by the door. They looked, well, they looked demonic. Big tongues hanging out. It looked like red leather, but somethin' was weird about it. I picked one up. It was wrinkled and old and smelled like storage. My first thought was that I should put it in the app. I'd love to know what I'd look like in it, mix and match some stuff Hot Topic maybe. Could be really neat for next year.

"Uh, dad?" Will said.

"Hmmm?"

"What are those?"

"Your masks."

"But what're they made of?"

"Put them on, son, and get into the woods. Hurry."

"What're we s'pose to do? Just scare 'em?" I asked. I think I made a face at the mask.

"This isn't your first time, is it?" he asked.

"Well, normally I'm looking for a nice boy to hang on to so he'll notice me. Kinda figure that's the wrong idea from this side."

Mr. Groyen laughed. "Very much so! Just scare them out of the woods. Maybe give your sistren a chance to get noticed."

"Right. . . ." I said.

He rushed us out. "Oh, and keep your masks on." He was earnest again. "Don't take them off. Wouldn't want the hunters to catch you."

We went back into the woods, Will and I. Somethin' felt different. The air was heavier. Maybe it was just the mask. The carnival lights shut down behind us. The hunt would start soon.

"Will, how are we s'pose to do this?"

"I don't know. Just scare folks, I guess."

"Where's the cake?"

"What cake?"

I stared at him. I think he stared back. It was hard to tell with the demon mask sticking its tongue out at me.

"What do you mean 'what cake?'"

"I don't have any cake."

"I meant the hunter's trophy."

"Oh, that cake. No idea. Dad hid it and no one's gonna find it."

"Why not?"

"You ever heard of anyone finding it?"

Then we heard voices. They were coming up the trail, going toward the clearing.

"Wanna bet they all scream?" I asked.

He nodded and we moved toward the voices. We were walkin' along beside the trail, real quiet, but needn't have been. They were loud. When we could see them, just barely the group split up. One of the kids had white pants that kinda glowed in the shadows and moonlight.

I pointed to the group with the kid in white and Will nodded. We stepped into the trail and started following them. There wasn't any light, except the Hunter's Moon. I stepped on a branch.

"Jake? Is that you?" One of them asked. It was a girl, I think.

"Jake, this isn't funny." Definitely a girl.

"Fine," Will said, changing his voice, and hurried forward to them.

"You're such a jerk, Jake."

Will was almost with them now.

"Yep, but this isn't Jake." He clicked on a phone light and the girls screamed. They ran back the way they came.

"That was easy," I said.

"Wanna get Jake? I can hear the guys over there."

I could barely see Will pointing.

"You don't want to? I ain't never heard you so happy."

"Kinda thought you might want payback for earlier."

"The asshole with the mouth was Jake?"

"Mmhmm."

"Lead me to him."

We walked toward the noise. It felt too easy, but also kinda exciting. What if someone recognized me? I'm not sure I was supposed to be anonymous, but the mask couldn't just be for scaring kids, right? Why not a little just desserts?

We caught up to the next group. All boys this time. Will went around them and made an owl call. I wasn't sure why that made my heartbeat speed up. It was so cheesy.

Anyway, I started running at the boys and yelling nonsense. Honestly, I'm just glad I didn't say somethin' stupid like "Fee fi fo fum."

The boys howled and ran down the trail. Will came up outta nowhere and they screeched like a buncha coyotes. They ran into each other before going their separate ways through the trees, screaming bloody murder. Well, most of 'em.

One stood stock still.

I went up to him. I could smell piss. The smell and darkness reminded me of waking up after a party back at school.

"Hey," Will said. "You alright?"

The boy didn't say anything. Didn't move either.

"Should one of us go for help?" Will asked.

"I don't know." I moved in front of the boy. He stood still. I waved a hand in front of him, but his eyes stared straight ahead.

"This is just weird," Will said.

A bluish light lit up the boy's face.

"Can you bring that light closer? I asked.

It got brighter.

"Thanks."

"Uh . . ."

"Is he alright?"

It wasn't Will.

I turned and saw a maglite bobbing up and down.

"Dad?" Will asked.

"My God, that's Mark Schmitt. Is he alright, Will?"

"Uh? I don't–Clare?" Will turned to me.

"Well, we don't rightly know, Mr. Groyen. He's . . . he's frozen."

"Frozen with fear," Mr. Groyen said.

I couldn't see his face good, but he sounded kinda happy. He wasn't worried like we were. I could see Will was scared.

"What do we do, dad?"

Mr. Groyen got up real close and shined his light in Mark's eyes. I could see both of them better now. Mr. Groyen had a mask like ours on.

"Oh, he'll be fine, son. Just fine."

He stepped back, appraising the boy. There was a purple flower pinned to the boy's shirt I hadn't seen before.

"Come on. Best he not wake up with us shining light in his face."

We followed Mr. Groyen a few yards away. He turned his flashlight off and we waited in the dark. I don't know how long it was. I remember Will asking if an armadillo was making that noise in the brush. His pa murmured an answer, so I took my mask off to hear better.

"Oh, hun, you shouldn't have done that."

Mr. Groyen turned on his flashlight and we saw Ma. Now, I seen Ma a lot of ways in my life. She weren't the same after she died and it took me maybe two days to notice. I never seen Ma this way before. She stood different, like a hunting dog that's got a scent. And her smile. Well, I thought only movie villains smiled like that. It was toothy and hungry and full not-love. She weren't my Ma then.

"What're you doing, hun? Come 'ere and let me look at ya. Did you get that from your app?"

Mr. Groyen hissed at me to put my mask back on.

"Well, come on, hun, let me see it. It doesn't go good with your costume." ·

I slid the mask back on and she glared at me. Hell, I didn't believe in ghosts or curses or none of that, but the look she gave me had me rethinkin' that position. Her skin was all pasty as she stepped towards us.

"Come on, hun. Let's go hunting."

"You're not my Ma," I said. I don't know why I said it, just that I did.

"What are you talkin' about? Didn't I raise you? Bake the cake for this hunt? No one else is gonna take you to it tonight, I guarantee it."

"Um, Clare?"

"What the hell, Will?" I asked, turning, but I saw it. Three others were there now. Not people. Jimmy was there, skin looking both tight and saggy on his frame. Miz Heusenfeld too and a banker I didn't really know. They had us surrounded.

"Where's my wife?" Mr. Groyen asked.

"What do you mean, Eli?" the banker asked.

"She went where the others went. Why didn't she come back?"

"Oh hun, not everyone gets to come back. We were the lucky ones is all. The Hunter's chosen few."

"Ma, what the fuck?"

"A young lady's got no business speakin' like that, Clare. 'Specially not to her mother."

"Good thing I ain't a lady," I said. "What's this superstitious talk about the Hunter?"

"Where did you think I came from, hun? Where we all came from?"

"Come and see," Miz Heusenfeld said.

"Come and hunt," the banker said.

"Where?" Mr. Groyen said.

Looking at the people who'd changed. I could only guess what happened to Ma and Jimmy, but they were both there on prom night. Jimmy with me when we seen that lady layin' on the side of the road and stopped to help. Ma runnin' out after Jimmy, wantin' to kill him for somethin' he didn't do when I came home alone and dirty. The others I couldn't guess what got them, but Pa's cancerous jokes about skin-walkers echoed in my memories.

I felt Will slip his hand into mine, cold and hard, but gentle. That kindness was what made me realize I didn't belong here, in this town. I wasn't like these people. I wasn't okay with any of this. The cycle of passive aggression and pride and whatever the hell these four were doin' in the woods at night. My greatest fear and my future. The same thing here. So I left. Will walked with me, his hand in mine. I guess I was too stressed to think about which hand was so heavy, but I remember having a certain clarity. A presence of mind that this was the only thing I could do.

Ma called out after me, and Jimmy stalked us for a while. At least I think it was Jimmy. I didn't turn around to look. Just kept walking all the way back to the festival. The lights had come back up when the kids returned so we slipped into the crowd. I took the truck back to Ma's house, packed my stuff and went back to college.

I kinda wish I had done something badass with the whip. I didn't even think about it. I knew what I had to do and, yeah, it was hard, but it was so much easier than staying. Sometimes, I guess, leavin's the best thing to do.

A Monstrous World: The Weird Fiction of Frank Belknap Long

Katherine Kerestman

FRANK BELKNAP LONG. *Library of Weird Fiction: Frank Belknap Long.* Edited by S. T. Joshi. Lakewood, CO: Centipede Press, 2022. 808 pp. $60 hc. ISBN: 9781613473009.

Frank Belknap Long was a prolific writer of weird fiction, science fiction, and detective stories whose career spanned most of the twentieth century. That he was a friend, colleague, and satellite of H. P. Lovecraft is often given as the reason for his lesser sort of renown, his own work being eclipsed by its proximity to the shadow of genius. In this new collection, S. T. Joshi has assembled a group of stories that highlights Long's important contributions to the genre of cosmic horror, focusing on Long's unique insights into humanity's role in the cosmos, as well as on his involvement in the development of Lovecraft's Cthulhu mythos, while representing his talents in multiple literary genres.

Much of the dark, cosmic horror in these tales is described in terms of Jungian archetypes: we are conceived with, not original sin, but genomes which are the repositories of our primeval fears. Before there was earth and there were humans, things existed, things which will exist long after earth and humans have passed away. These things are monstrous; they have no thought for us, any more than a mountain has when it crushes a climber in an avalanche of frozen water, rock, and soil. They have no feeling for us. They have no empathy. Their utter lack of interest in our habitat and our species implies our inability to move them to pity, to reason with them for any objective kind of good.

Long's stories are populated with more monsters than are dreamt of in most philosophies—mammal/reptile hybrids, twisted human killers, invaders from other dimensions, sea creatures, space creatures, subterranean creatures, devils, elder gods, and mad scientists—for whom humans and other life forces may be only a source of food or merely nuisances. Humans differ from these monsters only in their possession of moral insight and empathy. Well, maybe not. Long's protagonists, often learned in psychology and the sciences, question whether humans have the ability to understand more advanced forms of life—and they realize that one cannot judge that which is beyond one's comprehension without relying on unsupported assumptions. The suffering and destruction wrought by these more advanced life forms begs the question, meanwhile, of what exactly "more advanced" is.

In the posing of such ontological questions, reading Long is like watching *The Twilight Zone*—sometimes the moral is stated explicitly, sometimes implied. Long's style is literary, having a sophisticated diction and an expectancy that the reader will possess at least a minimal familiarity with ancient myths and history. His prose is fluid, elastic, and dread-evoking, foreshadowing something malevolent around every corner.

Fear, in these tales, is the nature of the human condition; our fears are instinctive, genetic—expressed as dreams, intuitions, and clairvoyance. Our fear of the environment pervades each tale—the habitat which spawned us threatens us, too. Radiation and atomic bombs pose significant threats, yet these dangers pale beside the primeval fears we know by virtue of the hereditary scars we carry in our genes from battles waged aeons ago. People experience another fear, too—a fear greater than the fear of losing our lives in a hostile world—the fear of losing our very selves. This fear of being co-opted by controlling alien intelligences is distilled in the story "Journey into Darkness": "in a world of hydrogen bombs and a technology that has gotten so far out of control that we could wake up tomorrow and look down over ourselves and discover that we've been transformed overnight into beautifully mechanized robots with pushbutton brains and built-in stimulus response circuits."

Scientific advancements have taught us how insignificant our species and our planet are, intensifying our instinctive fears. Again, from "Journey into Darkness": "Early man never journeyed into darkness with quite so terrible a burden of fear, for the myths which gave him some measure of protection were not combined with a conscious awareness of how cold and vast and dark the great prison of the universe actually is." Despite this omnipresent threat, people still try to achieve career and personal goals, fall in love, raise families. The result is a study in futility—the world of Frank Belknap Long.

Swordly and Sorcerous Adventures in Atlantis

Darrell Schweitzer

JOHN SHIRLEY. *A Sorcerer of Atlantis.* Hippocampus Press, 2021. 305 pp. $20.00 tpb. ISBN: 9781614983323.

It was as I was interviewing John Shirley for the current issue of *Startling Stories* that it occurred to me what a superb pulp writer John Shirley would have been. Not that he has written anything like Doc Savage or The Shadow, but he has written men's adventure novels, for all he is best known for transgressive horror and science fiction with a distinctly rebellious edge. But he has the major pulp virtues: clean, clear prose, vivid action, and the ability to keep a story moving. In a pulp story, things have to *happen*. The heroes have to *do* something.

A Sorcerer of Atlantis is a sword-and-sorcery novel in the tradition of Robert E. Howard and Fritz Leiber, and would certainly appeal to fans of those writers. Things certainly *happen* in its pages. We meet our two unlikely heroes being chased out of a cave in what can only be Clark Ashton Smith's Hyperborea by sub-human Voorhi. Brimm and Snoori have been pals since boyhood, for all they are quite different. Brimm is a tall, long-limbed, boyish-looking fellow who is nevertheless quite agile and quick with a sword. But he is most notably a half-trained, flunkout sorcerer, who was apprenticed to a master of that art but ultimately rejected. His knowledge of spells is sketchy at best. Snoori is a short, exceedingly hairy, barrel-shaped man with earthy appetites, who is probably more reckless than the intellectual Brimm. After their failed treasure-hunting expedition in the caverns of the Voorhi, the pair show an unending talent for getting into trouble, yet somehow surviving it. They decide to try their fortunes in Atlantis and take passage on a ship, only to be made galley slaves. But this doesn't last when Brimm is able to conjure a storm and wreck the ship on the shores of Atlantis, where the two of them attempt to take advantage of a standing offer to rescue a princess and instead find themselves tossed into a dungeon, then an arena, then offered in sacrifice to a demonic goddess. By the time they've worked free of that and become guards in the service of the Atlantean queen and her idiot husband, they've also gotten involved in a conflict that encompasses sorcerers, gods, Lovecraftian Deep Ones, and the fate of Atlantis. Cthulhu lurks in the background. I won't tell you how this works up to Romulus and Remus, but it does. There's also a warrior princess of Ur as a romantic interest. This everything-including-the-kitchen-sink approach works because Shirley is able to keep the action going at a frantic place and writes with clarity, invention, and considerable wit. The result, if not a profound epic to change your heart forever (which it is not intended to be) is vastly entertaining. In the good old days, this probably would have been a Lancer paperback with a Frazetta cover. That sort of book.

Also included in the volume is a more mystical or metaphysical novella, "A Prince in the Kingdom of Ghosts," which, frankly, I found less successful. A young man, whose father died mysteriously, is himself murdered and finds himself in a strange afterworld as created by a Chinese philosopher, where his father reigned as king for years before being mysteriously poisoned and left in suspended animation. (Yes, you can die for good in this afterworld, even though you are already dead.) The details are inventive. Our hero meets people ranging from Thorne Smith (the novelist) to Marcus Aurelius. But there is way too much lecture-tour explanation of things, and not enough plot development. The result is readable enough, but amid all the explanations of what it all means, not enough happens. Maybe it is not intended to be a pulp story, but whatever it is, it bogs down.

But the main attraction in this book is great stuff.

Feeding Nothing to Good Effect

Géza A. G. Reilly

CURTIS M. LAWSON. *The Envious Nothing: A Collection of Literary Ruin*. New York, NY: Hippocampus Press, 2022. 260 pp. $20.00 tpb. ISBN: 9781614983651.

Curtis M. Lawson seems well on his way to becoming a mainstay of the horror genre. His output is impressive: Since 2017, he has released five novels and novellas, three collections of short stories, and appeared in numerous anthologies and magazines. His most recent effort is *The Envious Nothing: A Collection of Literary Ruin*. Though I wasn't particularly impressed by Lawson's last collection, 2020's *Devil's Night*, I was happy to find that *The Envious Nothing* shows significant improvement.

The Envious Nothing contains seventeen stories and five poems. Hanging over the whole of the collection is the presentation of "nothing," the absence of something, as a palpable force that desires in some fashion. Often, the "nothing" is represented by hints or allusions to Angrbòda, the jötunn giantess mate of Loki and mother of his monstrous children. However, it is equally likely that the "nothing" will stand on its own, such as in the opening story, "You and I and the Envious Nothing," a science fiction narrative where the unexpected absence of the planet Earth is emblematic of the presence of the "nothing." What Lawson was driving at with this presence of absence I am not certain, but it is affectively engaging, and it does cast a pall of grief and foreboding over the whole of the collection.

Most of the stories present are successful and skillfully written, though I think that Lawson has some difficulty with pulling off wholly satisfying endings. The aforementioned "You and I and the Envious Nothing" is a strong start to the collection, and the second story, "The Witch of Rock Hollow," sends the reader into an inventive nested narrative about generational trauma and small-town ignorance with only a somewhat rushed ending to mar it. "Beneath the Emerald Sky," which appears much later in the collection, is a strong folk horror story that leans heavily on its fish-out-of-water characters to build an atmosphere of alienation and terror. Special attention must be drawn to "The Truth About Vampires," which is not only the best story I've read by Lawson but is also perhaps the best vampire narrative I've come across in well over a decade. Equally, "A Wordless Hymn" is a fascinating vignette that proves Lawson can cut loose from conventional forms and ideas when the inspiration takes him.

Other stories surprise the reader with their choice of character, location, or theme, adding to their strength. "The Happiest Place on Earth" is, as the title suggests, a gripping tale of an apocalypse at an amusement park with a conclusion that is satisfying if a bit confusing. "The Green Man of Freetown" is a deeply affective psychological portrait of loss and guilt. "Monsters Have No Place in the World That is to Come" is a shocking story about the last member of the Hitler Youth coming to a monstrous end–though I am unsure that the narrative would work outside of its place in this specific collection. "Elvis and Isolde" (a lovely title) is in much the same boat; though engagingly written, this dual-world story hinges a bit too much on the overarching presence of the "nothing" and Angrbòda. "Great-Uncle Bendix" avoids this pitfall, and it is a lively piece even though it suffers from sharing the overall "young couple move to a house in the country and encounter something evil" structure that is time-worn by now.

As my hedging might suggest, there are no real failures in *The Envious Nothing*. Even obvious parables like "Vermis Parandos" are well written and engaging. "Everything Smells Like Smoke Again" is a predictable tale, but it is fun for what it is. "Secrets of the Forbidden Kata" manages to take what seems at first blush like a very silly concept and transforms it into a powerful body horror tale. Even a Bradbury-esque story like "The Rye-Mother" has a wistfulness to it despite being rather insubstantial on the whole. "She Born of Naught" is similarly insubstantial, though it does play nicely with the idea of Angrbòda (who is not named in the piece) being the mother of monsters. The only story that really left me cold was "A

Grave at the End of the World," which is a shame because there is a skeleton of a strong narrative here, but it is hampered for me by some on-the-nose constructions and a conclusion that fits in with the overall theme of the collection but nevertheless feels unearned despite some rather hackneyed philosophy present.

I am unfamiliar with Lawson's poetry outside of *The Envious Nothing*, but it is obvious that he has placed pieces here to help the collection maintain the thematic direction that he wants to build in the reader's mind. "Angrbòda" sets the stage at the outset, and "White Night and Black Stars" reminded me of Robert Charles Wilson's outstanding short story "The Perseids" with its melancholy and theme. "Waspqueen Sestina" and "Thurisaz (in the negative aspect)" continue the trend, and "She Hunts Dying Monsters" rounds out the poetry present. That final poem is placed jarringly after "The Truth About Vampires," however, though it does lead nicely into "Beneath the Emerald Sky." I would be interested in reading more of Lawson's poetry, but here, I found them rather difficult to keep in mind as the stories surrounding them jump from location to location and concept to concept. This is not to say that the poems are not good works, but they are, ultimately, more garnish than meat.

The Envious Nothing is a strong effort, and it is head and shoulders above *Devil's Night*. As I said at the outset, Lawson is becoming a mainstay of the horror genre, and having already proven himself capable of producing exceptional novels (via 2019's *Black Heart Boys' Choir*), he seems to have turned his hand towards mastering the short story. I wouldn't say that he is quite there yet, but this collection is proof that he is well on his way. With its light-touch (but nevertheless impactful) thematic structure, its variety of approaches, and its tightness of prose, *The Envious Nothing* would be a fine addition to any reader's shelves.

Ask Leeman: An Interview with the Creator of *Ask Lovecraft*

Alex Houstoun

Life occurs at hyperspeed online. Websites launch and fold within weeks or months and creative projects are abandoned shortly after they are announced. Jokes and humorous content have even shorter lives, maybe a literal fifteen minutes of relevance before they are discarded and relegated to the trash bin of Internet culture. It is a constant, ceaseless, churn through content. Creating something that may last, that may be unique, even for a brief while, is an ever demanding, and draining, process to say nothing of actually finding and building an audience.

And yet, that is just what the YouTube series *Ask Lovecraft* has accomplished. Started in June 2012 by Leeman Kessler, *Ask Lovecraft* is a series in which Kessler plays a mysteriously resurrected H. P. Lovecraft who spends his time fielding all types of quesions as part of a video "advice" series. Over the course of a decade the show has grown and introduced new characters, bits, beats, and concepts, but at its core, the premise is simply Howard Phillips Lovecraft answers a question in the course of a two- to five-minute video; that's it. But that's not it.

Ask Lovecraft, in and of itself, is not a joke although Lovecraft's answers often are humorous—to say nothing of subsequent supporting characters such as evil twin P. H. Lovecraft. Rather, it provides a weird place of reflection in which Lovecraft, the fictional character, incorporates real aspects of his life and work while applying them to topics and subjects Lovecraft, the person, could never have addressed. There is a thoughtfulness, curiosity, and enthusiasm to Kessler's Lovecraft that is both reflective of the better parts of the real Lovecraft and the amount of care and work Kessler has put into the series since launching it. On top of the work Kessler has invested in his character(s), he maintained a rigorous schedule of publishing new videos, consistently updating every week since launching, for a majority of those years three times a week.

In January of this year, Kessler announced that the regularly scheduled episodes of *Ask Lovecraft* would end in June—an honest decade from when the series began. He was kind enough to take some time from his demanding schedule—on top of multiple creative projects and parenting two small children, he serves as the mayor of Gambier, Ohio—to discuss his creative process, the legacy of *Ask Lovecraft*, and what the future may hold.

AH: I have seen, heard, and read *Ask Lovecraft* described as a Q&A show in which a resurrected H. P. Lovecraft answers questions from an unknown audience for unknown reasons. While this is accurate, I don't think such a description really does justice to what the show is. Maybe it started there, but it certainly has a mythos of its own now . . . How did you describe *Ask Lovecraft* when first starting out in 2012 and how would you, looking back, describe the show's evolution or transformation with the years?

LK: When I started *Ask Lovecraft* I was a huge fan of the comedy advice series *My Brother My Brother and Me* (and I remain one still), so as I was poking around for concepts, the idea of dispensing questionable advice as Lovecraft struck me as something that would be fun to try out. The Internet is filled with abandoned Leeman projects from *Lies I Want to Tell My Children, Judging Creation, The Arkham Horror Book Club,* and on and on. So when I began filming *Ask Lovecraft* my hope was to do it for a while, but I had it in the back of my head that it probably would likewise fall by the wayside when something else struck my fancy; and yet here we are ten years later and part of that longevity I think comes from my willingness to follow odd trains of thought and let the show change and mutate over time.

So much of that change happened gradually that it was only when I discovered I had a TV Tropes site that I realized just how many odd directions I had taken the show in over the years. Introducing new characters like PH, Sagan, Chaboi, and even hapless producer Leeman allowed me to play not only with different voices but allowed me to juxtapose those voices with each other and explore the combinations that allowed. Adding *After Dark* as a fun sister-program let me take the mask off and play in the weird fiction/art space in incredibly new and refreshing ways. The base description of the show still hasn't really changed in ten years—it's still a comedy advice series starring H. P. Lovecraft; but from doing musical episodes to playing games to interviewing talented artists and writers, I've allowed myself to revel in the sense of play and keep it interesting over the decade.

AH: Do you think some of the longevity of the project may have had to do with Lovecraft as a source material? His life and work does seem like it would allow one to indulge some odd trains of thought . . .

If I am not mistaken, your greater introduction to Lovecraft and his work came after you were cast to play him in a play, correct? I can only imagine what it must have been like to approach him first as, you know, an actual person and then dive deeper into his fiction, his life, his letters, etc.

LK: I came to Lovecraft late. I was aware of Cthulhu and mythos-ephemera thanks to the Illuminati card game, The Real Ghostbusters, the Call of Cthulhu role-playing game and whatnot, but I was in my mid-twenties when I first started reading him and he was fine? I read *At the Mountains of Madness* and a couple of collections and I got why folks found him so inspiring, but I wasn't deeply gripped. Then in 2010 my friend Stephen Near asked me to play Lovecraft in a short piece he had written about Lovecraft's brief marriage to Sonia Greene. That play was expanded in 2011 and I reprised the role and I found both productions so inspiring that the following summer I picked up my flip cam and began filming.

I had done some research for *Monstrous Invisible* but depended heavily on the work Stephen had done. His writing captured the complexity and humanity of Lovecraft and it was a very useful jumping off point. At the start of *Ask Lovecraft,* my caricature of the man was more stylized and based on his writings. If you go back and watch those episodes, they are darker and meaner and more intense. It wasn't until an afternoon when I visited the Toronto Public Library's Merril Collection and began reading through their copy of *Essential Solitude: The Letters of H. P. Lovecraft and August Derleth* that I realized just how little I really knew of the man. In those letters I found his sense of humor, his self-deprecation, and idiosyncrasies which have gone a long way to inform my portrayal of him over the years.

I do think there is a big difference between approaching Lovecraft as an actor and as a reader or fan. It helps me to be able to wrestle some of the more difficult aspects of his life and his legacy. I get asked quite a bit how I can be comfortable portraying a white supremacist and it's something I've asked myself and written and talked publicly about at great length but ultimately, approaching Lovecraft as a character really helps in terms of thinking of him as a whole person. No one asks why someone might want to portray Iago or Macbeth or any other stage villain; we get that playing and exploring complicated characters is part of the appeal of acting. When it comes to historical figures, things get trickier, but I think the same motivations apply. I come not to praise Lovecraft but to portray him or something like it. While I recognize that my version of him is not a perfect facsimile—you never go full Lovecraft—this homunculus that I've crafted allows me to explore the contradictions and humanity of this literary figure and my hope is that in so doing, I enrich people's understanding of his life and his work.

AH: I would be remiss not to mention, and encourage our readers to read, a very thoughtful piece you wrote in 2015, "On Portraying a White Supremacist" (tinyurl.com/y4vcfctw). I find your closing paragraph to be brutally honest, and rather commendable, summation of the world you, and *Ask Lovecraft,* exist in:

> . . . the real answer is that I can only portray Lovecraft, warts and all, by being brutally honest about his problems and being willing to engage with it without throwing up defensive walls or complaining that the evergreen topic needs to die already. As new people discover Lovecraft, eventually his white supremacy is going to show itself . . . As long as I take money

for playing Lovecraft or accept invitations to conventions or festivals, I think it is my moral duty to stare unflinchingly at the unpleasantness and be willing to answer this question as many times as it takes.

You'll have to forgive me if I shift the topic away from the evergreen topic and spare us both another round of The Discourse because I did want to focus on another detail present in both your answer and in this essay. You mention Lovecraft's humor and the idiosyncrasies of his character on display in his letters to Derleth, and in general, and in the essay you briefly touch upon the creation of Lovecraft's Evil Twin PH as a useful means of tackling some topics that would seem out of character for Lovecraft—you've also already alluded to the larger *Ask Lovecraft* universe with the existence of Sagan, Chaboi, and producer Leeman.

I suppose the question I am working toward is one of artistic intent and vision . . . I am curious about your creation and development of the *Ask Lovecraft* "mythos," or other characters, and how you view them in relation to Lovecraft. PH may have initially served as a "cheat" to address matters in a way that Lovecraft would not, but I don't think that is all that he is. More so, as you continued to learn about Lovecraft as a person and discover both his evolution/growth as a person and the fact that there was a great deal of warmth and humor and, perhaps thanks to the sheer volume of letters he wrote, a whole range of Lovecraft personas, did it ever feel as if the show could have been contained to Lovecraft alone? I feel like in even asking this I am displaying my own lack of artistic vision or comprehension of the creative process.

LK: I started *Ask Lovecraft* in June of 2012 and that August I took a vacation where I didn't shave, much to the annoyance of my wife. When I got home, I had a whim and shaved all but a mustache and beard and filmed "The Real Lovecraft" (tinyurl.com/bdzjjsyv). This was the introduction of PH, who in the last decade has become a comic foil, a voice of conscience, and occasional book reviewer but who started off as an off-handed Star Trek Mirrorverse joke.

I feel as if that goes a long way to explain my creative process. I get struck by a whim, I follow it, and then it takes on a life of its own. I can't swear to it, but I would bet I only introduced Carl Sagan as a character because either I found a turtleneck at a Goodwill or needed a haircut and decided to have some fun first.

As for whether I could have avoided all the cheap gimmicks and side characters and stuck wholly to Lovecraft himself, it's impossible to say. Maybe if I had only committed to doing one episode a week. Deciding out of the gate that I was going to produce episodes every Monday, Wednesday, and Friday meant I had to come up with ideas fast and that I was a lot more willing to experiment in order to meet my schedule.

AH: Your original update schedule was impressive and I cannot imagine how demanding it must have been creatively—to say nothing of the sheer amount of time spent shooting, editing, uploading, and such—I cannot believe you were creating so much until 2019!

I must say I find it peculiar that you have described so much of this show as a following of, or indulging in, whims. I would be hard pressed to name any of my own whims that have resulted in a multi-day project let alone something spanning a decade. At the start of this year you announced that you would be retiring *Ask Lovecraft* in June, explaining, in addition to the demands of parenthood and your work in local politics, that you felt you had found "the limits of my niche." Would you mind elaborating on what it meant to find these limits? Did you feel that you no longer had whims to indulge or that the premise, characters, and world of *Ask Lovecraft* was reaching a creative limit?

LK: There's an economic calculation of input to output that needs acknowledging in projects like this. I designed *Ask Lovecraft* to have a fairly low input knowing my own mental and creative limits. When I started in 2012, I was not a parent or in local politics, but I was working full time at a bookstore and was engaged in various theatrical endeavors, so if I was going to add something new it couldn't be too taxing or my natural instinct to shelve the project and move on would be triggered. What I came up with was a system that was low-impact in its own distinct pieces but taken as a whole and looking back was an immense expenditure of time and energy.

Here's how my week broke down: Saturday night I'd go through my emails looking for a question not too similar to one I had recently answered or was sent in by a viewer whose question I had recently answered. I'd bounce the question in my head as I went to bed, making sure I could hit one or two interesting beats. Sunday morning I'd get up and continue working through those beats in my head in the shower until I had something solid enough to put in front of the camera. At some point, I'd suit up and get the camera out. In the early days I had a bedsheet I'd tape up to the wall and getting that monster to cooperate took up most of my emotional energy. Eventually I realized I could film in front of a bookshelf and that required a lot less work and looked much better.

Barring special episodes with multiple characters or locations, I filmed in one shot from start to finish based on the beats I had worked out in my head but really improvising. If I flubbed, I started over, and so it could take anywhere from one to dozens of takes depending on the complexity of the answer. A big part of sticking to one take was to keep from having to do a lot of editing. I recognized that I was much more willing to just film take after take after take than I was to sit hunched in front of iMovie stitching together the perfect episode. Once I had something I could live with, I "edited," which largely meant snipping off the beginning and end and making sure my fly wasn't open or my dog had wandered onto the set. I'd upload it to YouTube and set it to go public after midnight and then Monday I'd start sharing it on various social media pages. Monday evening, I'd go looking through emails and the cycle would continue with filming, editing, and uploading on Tuesday and Thursday and brainstorming on Wednesday and the following Saturday. Friday to Saturday evening was my mental break from the show.

That was my schedule for seven years with occasional breaks and vacations covered by filming a buffer ahead of time (which I foolishly never did during the regular run for reasons I leave to the imagination of your reader) or by filming live shows and splitting them up to cover the time. As I got more involved in my community and we added a new kid, I began to debate if I could keep it up and if I should hang things up or try to keep going. I had seen my number of subscribers plateau and while I was very appreciative of the folks who supported my Patreon and came out to my live shows, the rate of return for the energy and time I was pumping in was starting to diminish. This was also after I had added to my load by introducing *Ask Lovecraft After Dark* back in 2018 with my very first interview being with a certain brash lad by the name of Alex Houstoun. Given all these changes, by September of 2019 I announced that I would be going down to one episode a week, which gave me the breathing room I needed to continue doing the show for another three years. Given how 2020 went down, I'd say the timing was more than fortuitous.

Another fortunate timing was going on TikTok last year. I found that I enjoyed the format and the community of that app and was having a good time filming whatever came into my head from politics to Lovecraft to moss. Then in December I made a video about how I was winding down *Ask Lovecraft* and all the complex feelings I had about it and the very next video I filmed (on a whim) has gone on to have millions of views, prompted multiple media interviews and stories about my *Always Has Been* compendium of weird Ohio lore and suggested just what my post–*Ask Lovecraft* creative world might look like. That I named my account MayorLovecraft suggests that I'm not quite done with the old gentleman, but regardless it has been and continues to be a complete whirlwind and I'm both excited and nervous about where it will go.

AH: You mention "community" a few times: the community you live in, the community of *Ask Lovecraft* patrons, and the community of TikTok.

We first met in 2013 at NecronomiCon Providence and were both on a panel simply titled "HPL Online" along with Mike Davis of the Lovecraft eZine and Chad Fifer of H. P. Podcraft. All three of you were involved in creative Lovecraftian projects online in which your real name and opinions were available, if not directly interwoven, with your work. In contrast, I maintained a Facebook "author" page for Lovecraft (www.facebook.com/HPLovecraftAuthor/) and took pains never to acknowledge who was posting as Lovecraft despite how unprofessional or out of character I would sometimes behave.

I bring this up because something that stuck with me from that panel—particularly nearly a decade later when I view the Internet largely as a tool to drive people insane and/or con them out of money—is that a recurring point made was y'all saying, "I have put something out into the wildness of the Internet and it has connected me to others." It is simple in a sense but also profound.

Can you talk about the importance community has played with *Ask Lovecraft* and your (creative) work generally? While *Ask Lovecraft* or *Always Has Been* may start on a whim, are these whims or ideas that are meant only for Leeman or is the hope or expectation to reach someone else?

LK: What came to mind when you asked about community is the response I saw to the recent loss of both Wilum Pugmire and Joe Pulver. In the midst of endless debates and outrages, the outpouring of devotion and support spoke to the tangible reality of this community and the powerful good it can do. Both Wilum and Joe were incredibly supportive to me in my early days of filming. I remember Wilum posting a video (tinyurl.com/5cf3uak6) within just a few weeks of my first episode and it was my first taste of community support. As I mentioned, a lot of time this community can feel like a major source of drama, particularly when contentious issues arise or some brouhaha goes down at a convention or someone's book gets published but someone else's didn't, etc. etc. There can be genuine meanness and social media often rewards the negativity. Lord knows I've both been impacted by it and contributed to it in turn.

It is an odd thing to get grafted onto a community and to play catch-up on all the hidden rules and unsaid understandings. I came to Lovecraftiana or the Weird Fiction World or whatever you want to call it in a very orthogonal way. I was an actor who had discovered a fascinating role and wanted to explore it and I naturally needed to sell it to a built-in fanbase and community, and so I arrived as an outsider (wink wink) and it took some time for me to figure out just what my place was. I liked Lovecraft and Lovecraft ephemera but I wasn't a fan, not in the real sense. I didn't go out of my way to read his stuff, I didn't check out every movie adaptation or back every squamous Kickstarter. I made a lot of mistakes and presumed many things and I still do. However, it connected me with you and we have had a very pleasant relationship largely predicated on our mutual interest in Old Grandpa; we nevertheless discovered a real mutual respect and fondness and that pattern has repeated again and again with so many folks in this world. People I've only met virtually or briefly at various cons or gatherings are now quite near and dear to me and as an extrovert always craving friendships, that's a fantastic thing to experience.

Boundaries are important to anyone who's going to create on the Internet but there are moments when the guard can come down and genuine connection can be made and you are reminded about the deeply human reality of those people behind the screen-names and profile pictures. I had the profound fortune to get to actually spend time with both Wilum and Joe and got to understand just why they meant so much to people, beyond just their words and their online personas. They were caring, nurturing artists and they took time for people and for that, and the ways they made the Lovecraftian world a rich and real community, I'll always be grateful.

AH: So, am I correct in summarizing that the best thing that has happened in the last decade of Lovecraftiana for you was meeting me?

Awful joke aside, I would like to focus for a moment or two on *Always Has Been,* your "series" on TikTok. You may have come to Lovecraft and weird fiction from an Euclidean angle but *Always Has Been* strongly suggests that something of it made a lasting impression (or you have been hopelessly corrupted). I am going to sound incredibly old and out of touch as I describe the format of a TikTok video, but I really enjoy the format you've created: the videos feature you, filming on your phone talking to an audience, and you begin with "One of the nice/best things about living in Ohio . . ." and from there it truly is a mystery where we might end up. You rose to Internet fame with "One of the best things about living in Ohio is knowing that the Raven Queen won't ever set foot here. Not again. Not after last time." In that viral video, you appear to be simply walking in a neighborhood or a bit of forest. In other videos the location is more intentional: you stand in front of a frozen lake with a man "trapped in stone" in the center or you give praise to "the unfinished tower" at a construction site (?).

If *Ask Lovecraft* was improvised while you filmed, *Always Has Been* gives an even stronger impression of improvisation or spontaneity. It is hard not to view the videos as the recordings of a local man out on his walk who suddenly remembers something about why he likes Ohio so much; on a walk along the water he suddenly stops, thinks, and pulls out his phone: "One of the nice things about living in Ohio is that if you stand long enough on the correct side of one of our many beautiful rivers and waterways, you'll begin to hear the true secrets and lore of this land. However, I must caution you: if you stand on the wrong side, all you'll get are half-remembered dreams from those who have left Ohio. Figuring out which side you're on can be the work of a lifetime."

How did *Always Has Been* come to be and is the creative process similar to *Ask Lovecraft*? More so, while your TikTok username is MayorLovecraft, do you view the project as something directly inspired by Lovecraft? I ask that question knowing full well how obnoxious it can be to have an entire genre or range of stories and artistic effects boiled down to a single spooky guy.

LK: Alex, getting to know you and being subsequently Dread Pirate Robertsed by you into running the "official" Lovecraft page has definitely been a career high, have no doubt. Top ten for sure.

As for how *Always Has Been* came about or where the ideas come from, I can't really say. I chose MayorLovecraft as a username because I wasn't really sure what I felt about TikTok at first and didn't want to just come right and be like I'M

LEEMAN KESSLER Y'ALL DEAL WITH IT, so I subtly went with a sobriquet based on the two things I'm most known for. That's actually proven really funny because a lot of people see it and assume it's some joke and then I'll post about wastewater levels and they go "Wait you're a real mayor?" and it cracks me up every dang time.

My first *Always Has Been* video was The Green Path (tinyurl.com/9yudcc27) and it truly was born out of sheer whimsy. I was out at this lovely educational environmental space run by the local college that has meadows and ponds and gardens. It's just a minute away, so I take my kids there quite frequently and I believe this was a brief jaunt before I needed to get my son to preschool, so as I was watching him have a childhood. I noticed the way the path between the grasses looked and was struck. I pulled out the camera and filmed and it did pretty good numbers, which warmed my attention-hungry heart.

And then the Raven Queen. I was taking trash down to the curb and as I was walking up, I suddenly had a thought. Pulling out my phone and awkwardly trudging up the incline of my driveway, I recorded a couple of takes and picked the one I liked best. As of this writing, it has over three million views, which, if I've done my calculations correctly, means that more people have watched that ten-second video than have watched ten years of *Ask Lovecraft*. I've got complicated feelings about that but mostly positive ones. I've been on the news and in newspapers for some of my municipal work, but the attention I've received for this has blown all that out of the water. I'm still trying to catch up with it all. I suspect I've got just a few seconds left in my fifteen minutes but luckily it's been a fun ride and if nothing surpasses this, I'm sure I'll be just fine. Of course I won't weep if there are indeed more worlds to conquer.

AH: Both *Always Has Been* and *Ask Lovecraft* have a bit of a funny relationship with the truth and our objective reality; that is really a dressed-up way of me saying that some people seem to have trouble recognizing them both as works of fiction. You had released a video of you as Lovecraft reciting Edgar Allan Poe's "The Raven" (tinyurl.com/2p85ru76) that garnered a decent amount of attention online albeit with some of the response being "I didn't know there were videos of Lovecr . . . HEY! That's not Lovecraft!" Similarly, with *Always Has Been,* some folks have been having fun playing and building in your Ohio Mythos, whereas others range from confused to frustrated to cheated that Google and other sources would suggest that the Raven Queen is not a real part of Ohio's history—that, maybe, you are making things up.

The nature and subject matter of *Always Has Been* allows for a much more blurry relationship with "the real world," but I have long felt that *Ask Lovecraft* toes a similar line. Yes, Lovecraft has not literally been resurrected to host a Q&A show and opine on things ranging from plushies to Warhol, but the character you have created and worked with for this decade feels like a reasonable or realistic aspect of Lovecraft. It's not all direct quotes from his various voluminous writing, but it often feels like a reasonable extension . . . not a lie or a complete fiction but something reasonable—realistic.

Is this gray area something you find yourself generally drawn towards as an actor and artist?

LK: I love ambiguity and what English majors refer to as liminal spaces. As a kid, I loved spinning in circles and closing my eyes and reveling in the uncertainty of where I was facing. I also enjoyed sitting by luggage carousels at the airport and reaching that point where it feels like the belt is standing still and the floor is moving. While current global events show that there is a limit to the enjoyment of uncertainty, in small controlled doses it can be quite a delight to explore and it's not a stretch to say that those impulses inform my artistic process.

AH: With the end of *Ask Lovecraft* looming—global catastrophe notwithstanding—has your creative approach changed at all? Are there any lingering ideas or concepts that you want to try before the show's close? Do you find yourself perhaps a little more relaxed with your standards or willing to push and bend the characters further than you have previously?

LK: One of the issues prompting the ending of regular production has been a sense that my creative engine light is flashing. It's been harder to get motivated to do some of the more experimental episodes; and because I'm only filming once a week, there is both this pressure to make sure that I do a Good Enough Job on that one, but at the same time it's harder to rev up in the same way when I was doing three and was, to some degree, always on. I'm still having fun and finding fun and creative ways to play with the characters and the ideas, but there's definitely a feeling that things are slowing down.

As for whether ending the show is prompting me to just go bonkers and end on some high-octane binge of wacky exuberance, all signs point to no. I have a few beats I want to hit and some farewell notes planned but other than that, I'm more than happy to let the show do what it's done and then waltz out the door gracefully. The reality is that I think it will be hard to completely quit, which is why I'm careful to talk about this year being the end of the Regular Production of the show, meaning the weekly schedule. My hope is that as travel becomes safer, I'll still find myself invited to bring *Ask Lovecraft*'s live show to various conventions and gatherings and find other occasions to put on the suit and goggle my eyes for the camera. For better or worse, I've bound myself to Lovecraft's brand and I think there will always be a place in my closet for that suit and tie and opportunities to pull it back out and find myself sliding into his flesh-mask for yet one more ride.

AH: Life on the Internet is such that each day brings a new meme or trend, or article or person to be mad at, and, before one has truly grappled with the content du jour, everyone is on to the next thing. At the same time, the Internet never truly seems to forget anything and a work can simply sit there waiting for a new audience to encounter it or an older one to recall it. How would you like *Ask Lovecraft* as a "regular production" of a decade to be remembered, if at all?

LK: I think about this a lot, particularly trying to imagine how my kids are gonna respond when they realize just how many hours their dad spent during their childhood dressing up as a dead racist horror writer. I think the best outcome is that it becomes this artifact that keeps being discovered by younger audiences while a subset of older folks have some sense of nostalgia, remembering this series as it aired live. If I can be thought of in a similar way to any other Internet icon, it would be the fondness folks have for Homestar Runner.

Ultimately, much like with Lovecraft himself, I have no control over my legacy. That will sort itself out and I can tie myself in knots hoping that people will be talking and writing about PH and Chaboi for decades to come; but I think for my own sanity I need to make peace with obscurity and take joy from the warm responses I've basked in over the decade and the tangible privileges I've enjoyed thanks to this show and its incredibly supportive audience.

AH: Absolutely incredible how many pleasant memories were triggered by reading the words "Homestar Runner" . . .

As we come to a close, are you reading anything special these days?

LK: I am finally trying to read all of Charles Stross's *The Atrocity Archives*. I started this years ago and I even met Charlie at the H. P. Lovecraft Film Festival in 2015 but never got all the way through, so I restarted and am plugging away. Kids plus COVID anxiety plus *gestures at everything* has made it harder for me to read but with us entering the Lenten season, maybe I will try to incorporate dedicated reading time as some sort of spirituality edifying discipline. Time will tell!

AH: Hah! Thank you so much for taking the time. Who knows? Maybe we won't have to wait too long for the first PH Con or Journal of Chaboi Studies . . .

LK: Fingers crossed!

Tales from the Sticks

The joey Zone

LEE BROWN COYE. *Scrying Stones & Dolmen & Others: Chips & Shavings 1963–1964*. Foreword by Mike Hunchback. Camillus, NY: Chiroptera Press, 2022. 78 pp. $36 tpb. limited edition.

> Scrawny and thin my dead come in
> But looks are soon forgotten.

With respect to Ye Grizzled Shade, we can never unsee your art, Lee Brown Coye. The dermatology of a typical Coye (1907-1981) personage—revenant or living—is reminiscent of twisted sunbaked roadkill. His construction of architecture is all ingrown and fuzzy, the surrounding landscapes subscribing to a Wilmarthian permaculture. Lee's influence can be deduced in superlative modern-day scratches with gleeful grue of GUCKER or the feathery shadows of FELTON. But there is only one COYE.

The cover of this newest Chiroptera Press offering is one of his most brutal table settings: "Murgunstrumm's Work Room" from the title tale of Hugh B. Cave's Carcosa collection of 1977. This wrapper belies its contents however—here be a quieter creep. Words etching a stillness unnerving:

> Sometimes—minutes or hours later—a terrible silence woke him and he jumped from his chair. He looked at the clock. It had stopped and the tick sound was gone . . . The peepers had stopped and though he could see the splash of rain against the window there was no patter. The kerosene lamp burned but dimly. The wind had gone down and he hung shivering in a vast nothing.

The eighteen stories comprising *Scrying Stones* are accurately described in the publisher's prospectus as "less literary fictions than they are examples of American folklore" from "a time of horse drawn hearses and handmade coffins." Coye could be properly classified therefore as a Regionalist, much like Lovecraft. Ten stories had been previously transmitted audibly in the Cadabra Record releases *Where Is Abby? & Other Tales* and *Scrying Stones & Dolmen* (2015 and 2018 respectively). These were read by Lee's son, Robert Coye, who also corrected the texts in this volume before his death in June 2021. All had originally appeared as "Chips & Shavings" columns of the local *Mid-York Weekly*.

A grizzled shade and a friend. Portrait by Allen Koszowski.

Four "Shavings" previously unseen or heard since original publication are: "The Black Dog," a surprisingly sweet tale of a dog showing his owner where he should have been buried; "In Sight Fill My Soul," a version of the Phantom Hitchhiker folktale, getting you to take her to a dance first; "Three Steps and About Face," which describes the regimen of the ghost of a Continental soldier, albeit one only three feet high. Albeit just the mix of too many boilermakers with a dash of narrator; and "Spooked House," being a standout melodrama not dealing in the supernatural, with but "little need to fabricate the morbid when reality was harsh and grim enough."

The importance of this reprinted work is cemented by its title piece "Scrying Stones & Dolmen," a set of correspondence between Coye and others in something of a roman à clef including "John Vedder" [Vetter]; "Anthony Davis" [August Derleth]; and "Andrew Rothman" [Rothovius]. This regards weird geologic and wooden constructs glimpsed in Central New York's "Burnt Over District," "a belt of territory which seems to stretch along the length of the Erie Canal and toward the west that has been productive of many strange cults and beliefs."

Dead wood thus spoke to Lee Brown Coye and, as Mike Hunchback writes in his foreword, "he never stopped seeing those sticks in his mind, eventually drawing them over and over." A treatise on the omnipresent crescent moons in those drawings remains to be conjectured. Karl Edward Wagner based a story upon this "conversation"—"Sticks" appeared in Stuart Schiff's third issue of *Whispers* in 1974 (Here I might blasphemously proffer one of Stephen Fabian's better illustrations appended to the yarn where this reviewer first encountered it, in the first *Whispers* anthology collection of 1977). In a blur, *The Blair Witch Project* (1999) culturally appropriated those twig-formed sigils. For that matter, the code in J. H. Watson's treatise on the "Adventure of The Dancing Men" posits a runic predecessor.

The stories of Lee Brown Coye himself, however, will not only "live on through the long tradition of weird fiction small press adulation" but once read cannot be unseen. Nor in the posterity of print soon forgotten.

"It's the Beginning of the End": *Stranger Things 4*

Hank Wagner and Bev Vincent

Hank Wagner: So much to unpack here. So much fan service. So many homages. Where to begin?

Bev Vincent: How about with the obligatory opening statement of the Internet Era:

Warning! Here there be spoilers!

HW: Yes, for Vecna's sake, don't read this without watching Seasons 1 through 3. If only out of respect for the dearly departed. So, Bev, to start, thumbs up or down overall for the latest batch of episodes, appearing three years after Season 3?

BV: Has it really been that long? My, how time flies when you're having a pandemic. If you'd asked me that question after the first episode, my thumb probably would have wavered around the horizontal—a little up and a little down. Episode 1 was a bit of a slog, with its high school bullying drama that didn't seem important on the grander scale. However, as the season progressed, my thumb tilted strongly upward. The last two episodes in particular were brilliant, but there was much to credit in the middle episodes, too.

This season introduces the new "big bad," a creature in the upside down named Vecna, which is an anagram of the last name of Jack Vance, creator of a spell system for Dungeons & Dragons. We learn how Vecna came to be and what his master plan is—the destruction of the natural world so he can rule over whatever is left behind.

One of the braver choices this season, I thought, was keeping groups separate throughout. Let's start our discussion with group names to simplify matters. Team Russia = Joyce, Hopper, Murray, Dmitri (aka Enzo) and, to a lesser extent, Yuri, for example.

HW: I choose Team Scooby as the appellation for the California contingent, which included Joyce before she left for Russia to find Hopper. It also included Eleven, struggling to fit in to her new environs, before embarking on yet another hero's journey, this time to reignite her powers, seemingly exhausted after the battle at the shopping mall that ended Season 3. That team includes returning characters Will, Jonathan, and a new face, Argyle, a stoner endearingly portrayed by Eduardo Franco. In manner and attitude, Argyle bears a striking resemblance to Shaggy of Scooby-Doo fame. His pizza delivery van is a solid stand-in for the famed Mystery Machine. It also recalls another iconic vehicle from the eighties, the van driven by the A-Team.

BV: Every time he spoke, I was reminded of the late great comedian Norm Macdonald. Although he's mostly comic relief (he and Jonathan spend much of the season stoned, bringing to mind the dynamic duo of Cheech and Chong, and, later, Harold and Kumar), he proves to be most resourceful when the team needs to recreate Eleven's isolation tank.

Also, irrepressible computer geek Suzie gets to meet some of her long-distance friends face-to-face for the first time as she uses the lure of a 32-bit computer to assist in finding project NINA.

HW: Then there's Team Hawkins, consisting of Nancy, Steve, Dustin, Lucas, the irrepressible Erica, Max, Robin, and the new breakout character of Season 4, Dungeon Master Eddie Munson, portrayed by Joseph Quinn, who has a most—if not *the* most—compelling story arc of Season 4. Initially, I thought he might be this season's Billy Hargrove, but he turned out to be a much different character altogether. Another name for this squad could be Team Nancy Drew, as it's led by Nancy; the team also spends a lot of time exploring a haunted house once owned by a man named Victor Creel, played by Robert Englund, who, as most everyone knows, portrayed the infamous Freddie Krueger in Wes Craven's *A Nightmare on Elm Street* series. That's significant, given the *Nightmare* vibe present in much of Season 4.

BV: On a non-horror / non-upside-down level, the season was very much about finding a place in a new environment. Dustin befriends and defends Eddie, the heavy metal DND master drug dealer who is falsely accused of the first death in the season, and Lucas is trying to straddle the worlds of popularity as a bench-warming basketball player (who gets his chance to prove himself) and hanging out with his real friends. Eleven, always the outsider, is bullied, Mike is dealing with a long-distance relationship and Will is grappling with his sexual identity (although I have to confess, I misread that entirely). Nancy is trying to sort out her feelings for Jonathan and Steve. Max has emotional issues to deal with as a result of her brother's death last season, and is escaping into a world of music that will become one of the show's centerpieces. Music has always been a big part of the series, helping establish the timeline (although a few liberties are taken), but this season the Duffer Brothers have outdone themselves and, in the process, brought Kate Bush, Metallica, and, to a lesser extent, Journey (with a terrific remix of "Separate Lives") to the attention of new audiences.

HW: We also learned more about the currently depowered Eleven's backstory, via some flashbacks that showcased Dr. Martin Brenner (who is somewhat surprisingly still alive at the beginning of Season 4 after being attacked by a demigorgon in Season 3) and his numbered protégé's. Brenner has a theory that her powers are merely dormant and can reactivated by knocking down mental roadblocks she's created in her mind. He concludes that the best way to do this is to allow her to recover buried memories via several harrowing sessions that take place in a sensory deprivation tank (shades of another 80s classic, *Altered States*). Thus, we learn about her early experiences in using her powers, and about her relationships with the other residents of the Hawkins facility. And, most importantly, with members of its staff; we learn that one orderly, Henry Creel, was actually the first test subject to reside there, several years prior to Eleven's arrival. He's 001 to Eleven's 011. Henry's story turns out to be a critical piece of the puzzle surrounding the strange occurrences in Hawkins over the past several years. And, the house he grew up in is truly haunted; it also evokes Norman Bates' eerie homestead.

BV: We get to spend a lot more time in the upside-down itself, this season, learning a few of its secrets and mysteries. Plus, we're introduced to another of its horrifying denizens, demobats, which turn out to be sensitive to the presence of outsiders and attack in swarms, almost like white blood cells in the human body. Their existence means that Team Hawkins has to come up with some creative ways to distract them so they can reach their various objectives.

One of the more amusing bits of this season involves the way they enter the upside down through one of the increasing number of portals that are appearing in town—it involves a jury-rigged rope and a mattress, which is required because after climbing *up* into the interdimensional hole, they tumble *down* to the ground on the far side of the hole. It's visually fun and, at times, hilarious—when it isn't terrifying. The creators promise we will learn the truth about the upside-down in the final season. Where did it come from? Was it always there, just waiting for someone to break through into its Lovecraftian existence, or was it created at the moment in time at which it seems stuck?

HW: This season also had its share of social commentary as well. First, it was natural to have the USSR continue in their role as the embodiment of the "Evil Empire," given that the fall of the Berlin Wall and the so-called Soviet "Empire" were still three years in the future. The Russian aspect brought to mind a plethora of 80s films, like *Rocky IV* and *Red Dawn*, and any number of Chuck Norris vehicles. The Russian prison camp feels like a Hellmouth, due to its otherworldly denizens, and the unholy experiments going on there.

BV: For the most part, Hooper, Joyce, and Murray work in isolation from everyone else, with Hopper in prison in Kamchatka and Murray and Joyce teaming up to break him out. Hopper staged his own semi-successful escape, only to be sent back to prison. Then, after another daring escape (Shawshanklike in that they have to wade through miles of shit), they realize they have to break back in again to destroy the upside-down entities still in the prison, leading to a final confrontation with a demi-gorgon where Hopper wields the same sword Arnold Schwarzenegger used in *Conan the Barbarian*.

HW: David Harbour seems to be breaking out of Russian prisons quite regularly the past year or so; Scarlett Johansson broke him out of one well before Season 4 in Marvel Studios' *Black Widow*.

Veering back to social commentary, the show also fearlessly examined Satanic Panic (basketball captain Jason accuses Eddie of being the devil) and the kneejerk demonization of the Dungeons and Dragons crowd (a.k.a. The Hellfire Club, perhaps a nod to Peter Straub's novel of the same name, or to the X-men comics?), something that actually happened. That also made me think about Tipper Gore's assault on the First Amendment, via her criticisms of rock and roll lyrics.

Third, there was a lot of overt commentary about the Hell that is High School, as the young adults tried to fit in their respective school environments. Eleven's interactions with the mean girls who rule the roost at her school are heartbreaking, to say the least.

Finally, there were some sly jabs at the Midwest/Indiana lifestyle, reflected by how easily teenagers from varying factions were able to arm themselves at the War Zone army surplus store while pursuing their various agendas. Gun control? Ha!!

BV: The unexpected hero of the season (we all expect Eleven to be heroic, and she is) is Nancy. My favorite scene of the entire season is the determined look on Nancy's face when she shoulders that sawed-off shotgun and pumps round after round into Vecna. An intrepid reporter and amateur sleuth, she's also fierce.

BV: I found it interesting to learn that the pandemic delay meant the writers had all the scripts finished before filming started. If they discovered something interesting to explore later in the season, that meant they could go back and plant the seeds in earlier episodes, a luxury they aren't normally afforded. One example of that is the decision to have Eddie distract the demobats by playing Metallica's "Master of Puppets." Having come up with that scenario, they were able to write in the fact that Eddie played the guitar earlier in the season so it didn't come from the blue. I wonder how often showrunners write themselves into corners they can't fix because filming is already underway and they have to resort to some hand-wavey Deus ex machinas.

This season ends with Hawkins pretty much in ruins and people leaving town en masse. (I do wonder why anyone stuck around after some of the previous incidents.) Eleven's "defeat" of Vecna only seems to have made him stronger (a la Obi Wan Kenobi), as it appears that the Upside Down is encroaching on the real world. The final frames are truly haunting, intimating darker things to come.

Hank, where do you see things going in the final season? Are our heroes the only ones who stay in Hawkins to do what it takes to seal the rift? Will government forces be summoned to address this Lovecraftian phenomena? Can Hawkins ever heal from these seemingly fatal wounds? Seems like it could get really messy.

HW: Well, "Messy" is this show's middle name. I believe the Brothers Duffer promised some closure in the fifth and final season, so some plot contrivances might be in the works. I'd like to think they've been following a general road map of sorts throughout, while still surprising themselves along the way. This season definitely had the feeling of a very long middle installment, recalling *The Empire Strikes Back*, in that things don't look good for our heroes at this point. Will evil triumph?

BV: Maybe. This is a season where, despite several successes, our band of heroes ultimately failed at their objective and Vecna succeeded. And the body count this season was off the charts. Starting with cheerleader Chrissy and managing editor Fred. Ultimately, Jason and most of the Hawkins basketball team, virtually all of the Russian prisoners and then the guards, all of Brenner's team (and, likely, Brenner himself, not to mention revisiting the slaying of his original test subjects), Owens' team (possibly Owens, too), Sullivan's army, twenty-two people in Hawkins who died in the aftermath of the earthquake from the opening rift and, most tragically, Eddie Munson, who died an unknown (guitar) hero.

HW: There are certainly a plethora of open questions. How many more cameos can we expect? Will Hopper and Joyce consummate their love? Will Eggos still enjoy prominent product placement? Will we finally discover the final fate of fan favorite Barb? Are Eddie, Dr. Owens, and Dr. Brenner, really, truly, most sincerely dead? Does the appearance of a copy of Stephen King and Peter Straub's epic *The Talisman* in the final moments of the last episode have any relevance to the show, or is it just a Duffer Brothers Easter egg? Will Lieutenant Colonel Sullivan crack a smile? Will Dustin be forced to sing the theme to *The Neverending Story* again? Will Argyle remember to pass the dutchie 'pon the left-hand side? Who will Nancy pick—Jonathan or Steve? Will anybody besides Jonathan figure out that Will has feelings for Mike? Will Murray Bauman join the CIA or the NSA?

BV: Stay tuned!

Two from the British Library Archives

Karen Joan Kohoutek

MICHAEL WHEATLEY, ed. *The Horned God: Weird Tales of the Great God Pan*. London: British Library Press, 2022. 320 pp. $16.95 tpb. ISBN: 9780712354967.

MANON BURZ-LABRANDE, ed.. *Spectral Sounds: Unquiet Tales of Acoustic Weird*. London: British Library Press, 2022. 320 pp. $16.95 tpb. ISBN: 9780712354172.

Since 2018, the British Library has published over thirty volumes in their Tales of the Weird series. With their matching covers, monochromatic line illustrations on solid black backgrounds, green and purple this time, they look very nice on the shelf. Some of these publications collect the work of a single writer, but the majority bring together works on a specific theme, mixing well-known authors with otherwise unknown, sometimes anonymous ones. The selections are taken from the British Library's collections of older books and, particularly, newspapers and periodicals.

My personal interest in weird fiction probably peaks in the 1880s. This period immerses me in a very different time while also containing relatable modern elements, which gives it a unique frisson for me. I tend to find diminishing returns, that accelerate until my interest is almost completely gone by the 1930s, when the weird and uncanny was largely replaced by crime stories and realism (with exceptions, obviously). So this series usually hits my sweet spot perfectly, and these are two enjoyable additions.

Growing up, I read a lot of books about the Greek and Roman gods, with some Egyptian and Norse ones thrown in. Every time I came across a reference to Pan, I thought of a cake pan, or a frying pan. I didn't understand why a god would have such a mundane name. But unlike Apollo or Artemis, the goat-hoofed, devil-faced satyr wasn't very familiar to me, and as a god of fertility and the wild, I'd confuse him with Dionysus, although the former was more associated with shepherds and flocks and the latter with wine and vineyards.

In light of that, I found it interesting that many of the stories in *The Horned God* directly address the fading of Pan from the world, even if written at times when he had resurgences within popular culture. The publication dates range from 1860 to 1948, with the majority published in the 20th century, notably with distinct clusters of publications from the 1920s and 1940s. Several of the poems and stories were published in *Weird Tales*, which is something of an anomaly for this series, which tends to focus more on British publications.

After a poem by Oscar Wilde, the fiction kicks off, unsurprisingly, with Arthur Machen's "The Great God Pan," probably the most famous story on the subject for modern readers. Several big names follow, including Elizabeth Barrett Browning, E. M. Forster, Saki (H. H. Munro), and Kenneth Grahame, with a selection from *The Wind in the Willows*.

Pan is seen with a lot of different faces in these tales; sometimes sinister and dangerous, sometimes warm and life-affirming. Algernon Blackwood's story, "The Touch of Pan," came across as surprisingly prudish, judging the sexual freedom of the 1920s as shallow and artificial, even "rather nasty," in comparison to the somehow healthier, more natural sexual freedom of Pan's followers. In contrast, in Margery Lawrence's "How Pan Came to Little Ingleton," Pan stages a kind of intervention for an uptight clergyman, to get him out of his narrow-minded ways before he ruins his own life and the lives of his parishioners.

Both anthologies are strong in their own ways. *Spectral Sounds* is more of a classic Tales of the Weird assemblage, tending to the overtly uncanny. Under the umbrella theme of mysterious sounds, it includes overheard conversations, mysterious whispers, bells, rapping noises, and the sound of the kitchen coals being raked to start a fire, which is heard as an omen of death. These publication dates range from 1837 to 1920, with more than half from the 19th century, and Algernon Blackwood, Edith Wharton, and Edgar Allan Poe are among the most prominent contributors.

One of the pleasures of these anthologies is seeing what has changed, and how much, but how much has remained the same in society and in fiction, from the past to the present day. In *Spectral Sounds* we find that the trope of eminently rational, modern people, who disbelieve all superstition but are eventually forced to flee a haunted house, goes back a long time. It appears in Florence Marryat's 1883 tale "The Invisible Tenants of Rushmere," and the skeptical narrator facing the truly inexplicable also turns up in 1868's "The Day of My Death," by Elizabeth Stuart Phelps. The plot of either story could easily be updated to modern times.

A few of the stories, those by Poe and M. P. Shiel for example, are more fanciful and allegorical which, like some of the stories in *The Horned God*, expand the possibilities of the weird and what the category encompasses. *The Horned God* has more of that expansion, and more variety in style and genre. With its elements of allegory and fairy tale, its tone is a little more philosophical, even more melancholy, than the usual round of "weird."

Spectral Sounds contains more traditional ghost and supernatural tales, full of spiritualists, tragic marriages, and haunted lodging houses, representative of the classic era of British ghost stories. There's certainly room for both moods on my weird bookshelf. Honestly, the British Library Press can put out a hundred of these, and I'll read them all!

The World Fantasy Convention, New Orleans, November 3–6, 2022

As reported by Darrell Schweitzer

Full disclosure before we begin. Our Noble Editor has asked me to report on the 2022 World Fantasy Convention, from which I have recently returned (after a grueling 29-hour train ride, which was at least reliable in the way airlines are not these days); but I am in a rather awkward position to do so because I am a member of the Board of Directors of the aforesaid convention. (Of the WFC organization itself, which awards the annual franchises to the groups that put on the convention.) By the arcane and indescribable rites of said Board, I was affirmed into their company for another six years, after which time I will be 76 years old and no doubt ready for a gentle journey to the glue factory. But more than that I cannot say. I will neither confirm nor deny that the Board's secrets are zealously guarded by a special squad of thugees with ritual strangulation scarves. I certainly cannot criticize anything aspect of the convention itself. If I had any complaints, those are private, for the Board. Actually I don't have any complaints. I think it went splendidly. I had a great time. I managed to slip away for a few hours on Friday afternoon, hike down to the French Quarter, visit the Voodoo Museum, and renew my acquaintance with familiar sights, it having been 28 years since my last visit. It's still true that you get the cheap Voodoo dolls in the French Market, along Decatur Street. They cost $60 apiece at the Voodoo Museum, but I found some for $2.50 that I am sure work just as well. I got set of His and Hers dolls, with white pins, for good luck, which could well represent me and my wife. Someone at the convention said "I wonder about your intentions," but I assure you my intentions were entirely benevolent, even romantic.

But I digress. Back to the convention. Voodoo was a theme, for me at least, because I found myself on a panel called "New Orleans: Old Souls and New Rhythms," about the lore and literature of the place, and so I did my homework, and if they actually needed a Yankee to tell them about Marie Laveau, I was prepared to do so. (I also managed to talk about H. P. Lovecraft in New Orleans and forgotten New Orleans/*Weird Tales* writer Kirk Mashburn.)

What I actually can plausibly talk about is the aspects of the convention that pleased me:

First, that it happened at all. The pandemic is not quite over. Last year's convention in Montreal (which I intended to go to but missed because of border problems) was apparently very small, although by all reports, excellent. This year, attendance was reported to be about 500. The convention seemed well on its way to recovery. Health regulations were maintained. Everybody wore masks. I decided that if we had to wear masks, we should wear entertaining ones. As it was hot enough, even in November, for this to be (for me at least) more of a t-shirt convention than a coat-and-tie convention, I coordinated a Cthulhuoid t-shirt with a tentacled mask, and somewhat puncturing the dignity of the occasion, a Three Stooges mask some of the time. (But mostly tentacles.)

The convention had a nicely cosmopolitan attendance. Not only were there some people from the expected places, USA, Britain, Canada, etc., but Oghenechovwe Donald Ekpeki (from Nigeria) was present, as was Usman T. Malik (from Pakistan), in addition to toastmaster Ursula Vernon (who is great fun as a speaker), editor guest of honor Ginjer Buchanan, author guests of honor Jo Walton and Victor LaValle, artist Iris Compiet (from the Netherlands), "featured guest" Nisi Shawl, and special guests Brandon O'Brien (from Trinidad and Tobago), Andrei Codrescu (from Transylvania, though now resident in the US), and Caitlín R. Kiernan, who was apparently only in attendance virtually. Peter Beagle was there, and many other notables.

High quality programming. I got to some of the guest of honor interviews. I was on two panels, which seemed to go well. I particularly liked a "History of Fantasy Panel," with Edward James, David Sandner, Ginjer Buchanan, Gillian Polack (who participated virtually, from Australia), and Gary Wolfe, which could have been one more another publishing panel about how fantasy became a commercial genre, but instead delved into the multiple origins of fantastic literature itself and concluded that there was no single "origin," because different cultures have treated it differently. One unusual item I heard about later, but missed, was a demonstration of the art of falconry and a discussion of how to present such birds realistically in fiction, by Christine Avery, who brought along live falcons!

There were rare books in the dealers' room. There was a time when the WFC constituted a major antiquarian book fair. I remember one convention when two of the five known copies of Lovecraft's *The Shunned House,* as hand-bound by Robert Barlow in HPL's lifetime, were in the room, along with the only first edition of *The King in Yellow* in a dustjacket that I have ever seen. I am glad to see that sort of thing coming back. It has been a joke for years that it isn't really a WFC unless there are copies of *The Outsider and Others, Beyond the Wall of Sleep,* and Leah Bodine Drake's *A Hornbook for Witches* (one of the very rarest Arkham House books) on sale. This year had two out of three. (No *Beyond the Wall of Sleep.*) Somebody also had what was only the second copy of Lord Dunsany's incredibly scarce *A Glimpse from a Watchtower* that I have ever seen.

The food was great, not just generously served in the hospitality suite, but lavishly at the two main receptions, one after the Friday night mass-autographing, the other after the Saturday night art reception, with an emphasis on local delicacies: red beans and rice, various kinds of gumbo, jambalaya, etc. No need to run down to the Café du Monde and wait an hour to have expensive beignets. They had them at the receptions. I probably put on a couple pounds from my discovery of Mardi Gras King Cake.

Lots of good fellowship. I had pleasant, catch-up conversations with Adrian Simmons of *Heroic Fantasy Quarterly*, Gordon Van Gelder, and others. Ron Drummond let me page through a sample copy of the magnificent and much delayed "25th anniversary" edition of John Crowley's *Little, Big* that he had just published. I even did a little business, soliciting stories for an anthology I am editing.

I admit my bias, but this seemed a good convention all around.

About the Contributors

Ramsey Campbell is an English horror fiction writer, editor, and critic who has been writing for well over fifty years. He is frequently cited as one of the leading writers in the field. His website is www.ramseycampbell.com.

Alex Houstoun is a co-editor of *Dead Reckonings*. He has published *Copyright Questions and the Stories of H. P. Lovecraft*, available by contacting him at deadreckoningsjournal@gmail.com.

Katherine Kerestman is the author of *Creepy Cat's Macabre Travels: Prowling around Haunted Towers, Crumbling Castles, and Ghoulish Graveyards* (WordCrafts Press, 2020). She is wild about Dark Shadows and Twin Peaks, and has been seen frolicking in the graveyards of Salem on Halloween. You can keep up with her at www.creepycatlair.com.

Karen Joan Kohoutek, an independent scholar and poet, has published about weird fiction in various journals and literary websites. Recent and upcoming publications have been on subjects including the Gamera films, the Robert E. Howard/H. P. Lovecraft correspondence, folk magic in the novels of Ishmael Reed, and the proto-Gothic writer Charles Brockden Brown. She lives in Fargo, North Dakota.

Daniel Pietersen is the editor of *I Am Stone: The Gothic Weird Tales of R. Murray Gilchrist,* part of the British Library's Tales of the Weird series. He is also a regular guest lecturer for the Romancing the Gothic project.

June Pulliam teaches courses about slasher films and zombies at Louisiana State University in Baton Rouge, where she lives in an old house with multiple cats and dogs. She is the author of several books on subjects ranging from zombies to punk rock. When she is not dodging hurricanes, she paints.

Dr. Géza A. G. Reilly is a writer and critic with an interest in twentieth-century American genre literature. A Canadian expatriate, he now lives in the wilds of Florida with his wife, Andrea, and their cat, Mim.

CM Schneider is a jeweler, husband, father of three cats and one child.

A career-retrospective of **Darrell Schweitzer**'s short fiction was published by PS Publishing in two volumes in 2020. A veritable flood of Schweitzeriana is soon to follow from various publishers in the next year or so, including a new Lovecraftian anthology, *Shadows out of Time* (PS), *The Best of* Weird Tales: *The 1920s* (Centipede Press), *The Best of* Weird Tales *1924* (with John Betancourt, Wildside Press), a weird poetry collection, *Dancing Before Azathoth*, a new story collection, *The Children of Chorazin* (Hippocampus Press), and two further volumes of author interviews (Wildside Press). He was co-editor of *Weird Tales* between 1988 and 2007.

Joe Shea (The joey Zone) is an artist and illustrator. Samples of his work can be found at www.joeyzoneillustration.com.

Bev Vincent is the author of several non-fiction books, including *The Road to the Dark Tower and Stephen King: A Complete Exploration of His Work, Life, and Influences.* He co-edited the anthology *Flight or Fright with King* and has published over 120 stories, with appearances in *Ellery Queen's, Alfred Hitchcock's* and *Black Cat Mystery Magazines.* His work has been published in over twenty languages and nominated for the Stoker (twice), Edgar, Ignotus, and ITW Thriller Awards. To learn more, visit bevvincent.com

Hank Wagner is a respected critic and journalist. Among the many publications in which his work regularly appears are *Cemetery Dance* and *Mystery Scene*.